I Wonder What COLLEGE Is Like?

I Wonder What COLLEGE Is Like?

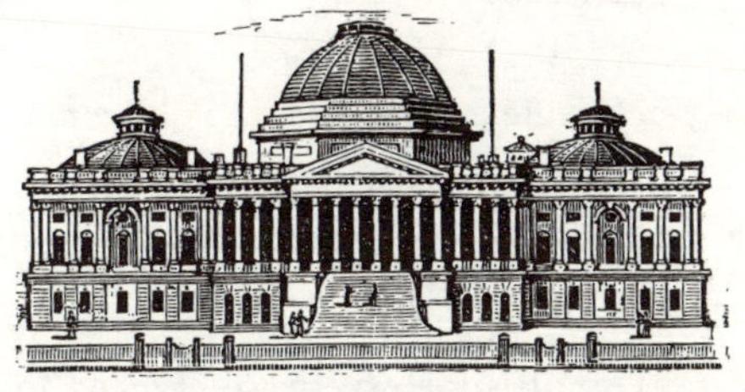

Meg F. Schneider

JULIAN MESSNER

Published by Julian Messner, a division of
Silver Burdett Press, Inc., Simon & Schuster, Inc.,
Prentice Hall Bldg., Englewood Cliffs, NJ 07632.

JULIAN MESSNER and colophon are trademarks of
Simon & Schuster, Inc. Design by Claire Counihan
Photo on page x courtesy of Nancy Walz/Wesleyan University.
Manufactured in the United States of America.
Library ed. 10 9 8 7 6 5 4 3 2 1
Paper ed. 10 9 8 7 6 5 4 3 2 1

Library of Congress Cataloging-in-Publication Data

Schneider, Meg F.
I wonder what college is like? / Meg Schneider.
p. cm.
Includes index.
Summary: Describes the experience of going to college, including the application and acceptance process, finances, roommates, socializing on campus, extracurricular activities, and living away from home.
1. College student orientation—United States—Juvenile literature. 2. Universities and colleges—United States—Admission—Juvenile literature. 3. College students—United States—Juvenile literature. 4. College, Choice of—United States—Juvenile literature. [1. College student orientation. 2. Universities and colleges—Admission. 3. College students. 4. College, Choice of.] I. Title.
LB2343.32.S35 1989
378.73—dc19

88-31189
CIP
AC

ISBN 0-671-65847-6 (lib. bdg.)
ISBN 0-671-67815-9 (pbk.)

To Adam and Josh.
Here's hoping you both
do what you want, and
that it makes you
happy.

ACKNOWLEDGMENT

I'd like to thank Larry Momo of Columbia University, Tom Keeding of Hunter College H.S., Fran Toliver of The Brearley School in New York, Ron Lynn of Stafford H.S. in Kansas, Dean Carl Polowczyk of Bronx Community College, countless staff members at various college admissions and financial aid offices, and the many college students who, with a lot of spirit, filled me in on the inspiring picture.

CONTENTS

♦ INTRODUCTION ♦

Why Is College Such a Big Deal?

Why is college such a big deal? The answer is simple. College is a big deal because it is a big experience that can change your life.

Chances are you've heard a lot about college. Your teachers may sometimes say, "You've got to work hard if you expect to get into college!" Your friends may passionately proclaim, "I can't wait to go away to college!" or "Ughh! Another four years in school after high school! Forget it!" And your parents may already be discussing schools with you or with an older sibling. The dinner table conversation may be dominated by talk of finances, careers, grades, SATs, and more.

People talk a lot about college because it is a whole new life experience. From the moment you begin to consider where to apply until the moment you receive your college diploma, you will be amazed to see how significant an adventure it really is.

The college years are a special time in your life because they are your chance to begin discovering who you are and what you can be. They offer an independence that encourages you to explore *you*. What classes interest you the most? What talent would you like to develop? How can you help pay for your own education? How much self-discipline do you have? Can you make a family of friends away from home? What dreams can you pursue . . . and catch?

College can be lonely and comforting, difficult and pleasurable, frustrating and rewarding, frightening and exciting. Some days may be filled with fun and success while others could spill over with disappointment and dejection.

Most big experiences are like that. They are filled with conflicting emotions, which can, as time goes on, turn you into a slightly different person—maybe a little wiser, perhaps a little stronger, and usually a lot happier and more fulfilled.

So if your teachers are beginning to echo the word *college* in your ears, and your friends are already worrying and wondering, and your home is strewn with your older brother's college catalogs, here is your chance to understand what the big deal is all about.

College is nothing to worry over. But it is something to appreciate and experience in a *big* way!

♦ CHAPTER ONE ♦

Is College Right for Everyone?

The college experience can give everyone something of value. But not everyone is ready to go. College is not just a big experience. It is also a big responsibility. The fact is, college is a very expensive and time-consuming choice. It's important not to waste it.

For some people college is a given. They simply assume they will go. Parents, siblings, and cousins have all attended. Going to college seems as natural as getting up in the morning. For others the path is not so clear. Maybe a sister or brother decided to pursue other options. Perhaps money problems or family responsibilities have made it hard to know whether college is in the future. Still others may simply feel too afraid, or unsure that college will get them where they want to go.

Is college right for you? Maybe yes, maybe no. Whatever you decide, it's important to know what to expect from the experience. Smart decisions are those made without fear or confusion.

The truth is, college is most "right" for those who are ready.

CAN I SUCCEED IN LIFE WITHOUT GOING TO COLLEGE?

First of all, *success* means different things to different people. There is no one way to succeed. What makes one person feel successful may not do the same for another. Feeling positive about yourself and the life you are leading generally brings a feeling of success. The question is, how do you get there? It's different for everyone.

You've probably heard that "to get a good job you need a good education." In fact, you may have heard it so many times that you're sick of it. Part of you may even be thinking, that can't be. There has to be another way!

The truth is, you do have to learn to do a job well. You can't just sit down and perform. But there are alternatives to four years in college. In fact there are a number of other ways to find a good job. Community colleges are one route. They offer two years of a sound general education. Graduates are awarded associate degrees in applied sciences (A.A.S.), the arts (A.A.), or science (A.S.), and can go on to pursue careers in many interesting fields. For instance, an associate degree in early childhood education can lead to a paraprofessional (assisting a professional) position in public schools, day care centers, and social service agencies. A business career specialization in accounting may lead graduates to jobs as bookkeepers, cost accounting clerks, and more. An associate degree may also pave the way toward a bachelor's degree (the four year B.A. or B.S.), or it may include certificate programs in such subjects as automotive technology or paralegal studies. The advantage of community or junior colleges, as they are sometimes called, is that they are relatively inexpensive, give students a chance to see how college feels, and offer degrees that can lead to good jobs. The disadvantage is that higher level positions usually require at least a bachelor's degree.

There are also a number of technical schools that offer programs in secretarial skills, data processing, electrical technology, beautician skills, plumbing, and similar fields. Some of these programs only offer the necessary skills to find an apprenticeship in your chosen field. This means you must work alongside a skilled or licensed person. Others prepare you directly for licensing exams, and still others help you land a good job immediately.

What you choose comes down to what you consider a "good job" and how you define success. It's important to ask yourself questions such as, "How do I see myself in life? What kinds of things would I like to do, and do I enjoy doing now. Do I need a college diploma to strive toward those things?" It's a little early for you to know all the answers, but it's never too soon to start dreaming.

Of course there are many people out there who are tremendously successful, both in terms of the money they make and the power they wield, who did not go to college. You might say, "Look at them! I can do it too."

And maybe you can. But it's important to remember that the world is increasingly competitive. As time goes by, it becomes harder and harder to make it without the right credentials. Those in artistic fields such as filmmakers, artists, and musicians probably find it easier to succeed without a college experience. But even in those areas, many of the most respected people have studied extensively in their fields.

Whether or not you decide to attend college, your decision should be based on knowledge, not on fear or misconceptions. Choosing beauty school or auto mechanics because deep in your heart you're afraid you'll fail at college is not a smart move. But following your burning desire to travel and see the world or concentrate on developing your carpentry skills is something else. It may be smart to follow your instincts. You'll get the most out of college when and if you want to be there.

College is one important first step on the road to finding yourself. Even if you can't foresee your future career, the new ideas you will gain from the college experience will have a profound effect on every aspect of your life. As you learn, your knowledge grows. As knowledge grows, your understanding of world events, people, and, most importantly, yourself will expand and will affect everything from your dinner table conversation to the way you raise your own children! A good education cannot help but broaden your life whether or not it starts you on a major career path. Life is filled with difficult and exciting choices. A college education can help you make the right decisions for you.

WHAT IF I GO, BUT IT'S TOO HARD?

When people say college is hard, they mean it has to be taken seriously. Unfortunately, many students think "hard" means "easy to fail." This isn't so. Not if you work hard and take responsibility for yourself. College is only easy to fail if you fail to take college seriously.

The decision to attend college is the decision to take on a confusion of possibilities. This is serious business. It's often easier to say, "I'm going to be an actress" or "I'm going to be a teacher," and simply pursue these avenues in a very focused, narrow way. But the truth is,

A lab course in cell biology is just one possibility for students with an interest in science. *Nancy Walz/Wesleyan University*

for the first year and a half, many colleges discourage this. Your college professors want your hard-working, eager, *open* mind. The college community as a whole wants your participation as an involved, concerned, changing, growing person.

The competitive spirit in colleges can be quite serious too. On some campuses it runs deeper than others. Watching others strive to be the best may be an inspiration for you. On the other hand, it may cause you a great deal of anxiety as you worry about how you will measure up. No matter how you react, those around you present a serious challenge to be the best you can be.

The professors in college demand that their students be serious about their work. They do not want to be babysitters. They expect that when they tell you to read something, even though there are no quizzes, you will indeed read it. The challenge is to motivate yourself from inside. You have to want to learn. Professors will not be checking up on you daily.

You are in a community of your peers. This means you are surrounded by kids your own age all of the time. There are no parents around to tell you what to do and how to do it. This can be wonderful fun, but it is also a very serious aspect of college life. How will you balance your social life, academic life, and community responsibilities? Now you will have to answer to your friends, professors, other significant people in the academic community, and most of all, yourself. You are your own responsibility.

Finally, it may be comforting to remember that you have been admitted to college by an experienced admissions staff. They've considered your high school grades, test scores, talents, interests, written application, interview, and recommendations, and have judged you able to do the work. They have given you a serious responsibility, but they have done so after much thought. If you can't completely trust in yourself, then have some faith in their judgment!

College is not "too" hard. It just cannot be taken lightly. College is there to help you succeed both before graduation and after. But college cannot do it alone. You have to help.

IS IT TRUE THAT COLLEGE WILL PREPARE ME FOR REAL LIFE?

There are many people who would say college does prepare you for real life. They might say that it gives you a chance to grow up and learn everything you need to launch a fabulous career. Some people even claim that employers everywhere are lining up to offer good jobs to good students from good schools.

However, most high school advisers, college counselors, and business professionals agree that for the most part this view of the college experience is not realistic.

While it is true that solid college credentials can play a big part in job hunting, college cannot prepare you for real life. This is because college is not like real life. At no other time in your life will you live in such close community with your peers. At no other time in your life will your most important concern be learning what you want to learn. And at no other time in your life will you get your first delicious taste of independence, or rather, dependence upon yourself alone.

Outdoor spaces at the University of California, Santa Cruz, provide a chance to talk or to sit and think. *Photo courtesy of the University of California, Santa Cruz*

What does college do for you? It frees your mind so that you are more able to greet life's challenges with some wisdom, knowledge, skills, creativity, and confidence.

The college experience is not like your first job. It helps you land the job. But chances are the nuts and bolts of the field you choose can only be learned on the job. College, however, is partly responsible for developing your ability to solve problems and come up with original ideas.

> I majored in English at a small Midwestern college and then came back East to find a job in publishing. Much to my disappointment, I began as a secretary. Anxiously I awaited my first small writing task. It took a while. My boss felt I had to learn the rest of my job before he would give me a chance at a creative assignment. Finally my chance came. I was to try writing some back cover copy for a new novel. Excitedly I sped through the novel and whipped out a page of beautifully written prose. My boss read it, called me into his office, and said, "Lisa, this is elegantly written. I think you have some terrific ideas here. But it doesn't work. Let me tell you why." Sick at heart, I listened to his criticism. That night I went home and read what I had done, keeping in mind my boss's advice. I began to see I'd expressed myself well, but the copy needed more. I had to catch people's eyes. I had to write something that made them wonder about the surprises in the plot. I worked for hours on another draft that night, changed a few more passages over the next two days, and finally handed it in. My boss took one look, smiled, and said, "O.K.! Good for you. Now we've got something to work with!"

The college experience does not teach you how to build a career. That is something you have to figure out in your chosen field once you are in the door. Rather, it is responsible in part for how you mastermind your moves up the career ladder . . . how you seize opportunities as you did in college to learn and grow independently.

> I had been working as an assistant to an account executive at a major advertising agency. At first I'd been thrilled to land the job, but it was over a year, and I still hadn't been invited to get involved in any important campaigns. Mostly I was responsible for coordinating all the different departments. It was my job, among other things, to make sure the art department got the latest text from the copy department and that the copy was approved by the executives in charge of the accounts. One day however, I heard my boss and the art director talking about a client. They were discussing the fact that they just couldn't come up with the right line for the new brand of ice cream. That night, feeling as I used to when going to the library to prove a point in a college paper, I went to a series of grocery stores. I took notes on what all the cartons had in common and what made each one special. Every night for a week I played with words and images to come up with the right combination, and when I was finally satisfied I got up all my courage and brought my ideas in to the boss. It wasn't great but it had something, and after all the heads of the departments got together to contribute their expertise, a solution was found! A few months later I was promoted.

And the college experience does not teach you how to handle adult relationships in the real world. Choosing your own friends, marrying, and having children is not like living in a dorm or off campus with a group of other students. Life presents us with many responsibilities that college can often shield us from. In college our priorities are clear. In real life they can become confused and difficult to balance. But seeing how much you affect those around you and how much you can depend on each other is a key to finding a place for yourself in a community.

> I had been living in the city on my own for several years when I fell in love. We dated for a while and then became engaged. It was an exciting time. One evening on my way back from work, I noticed my neighbor hobbling into his apartment. Quickly I walked over to help him in with his packages. He'd just broken his leg on a ski trip. Checking my watch, I noticed I was late for an evening with my fiancé, but instead of hurrying out of my neighbor's apartment, I called to say I'd be late and then lingered about twenty minutes helping to put away his purchases. It felt good. A little like being at college when all the kids would gather around a friend who really needed help. Before that experience everyone had depended on their parents. It had been wonderful to learn we could depend on each other . . . that each of us had the power to be as comforting and supportive as our own families could be.

Not everyone should go to college. Some people with very special talents will want to pursue them independently. Some people are simply not ready to face the rigorous responsibilities of school. They need a few years in the real world to feel ready to take college on. Others would prefer simply to take jobs and earn enough money to travel or do other things they want. They are comfortable with putting off decisions about the future.

But whatever you decide to do, it is a mistake to ignore the importance of an education both for yourself and the world you live in. Education can open up our minds so that what we do with our lives might be good not just for ourselves but for everyone.

♦ CHAPTER TWO ♦

Which One? There Are So Many!

Fortunately for you, there are thousands of colleges in this country that are worth attending. Unfortunately, you can't enroll in all of them! Your task will be to select the ones that, on the most important issues, suit your needs. This may not be easy, but it is an interesting and exciting process. There are many sources from which to find out everything you need to know about specific colleges. Think of it as detective work and enjoy yourself. The only thing you will have to consider is *you!*

You begin your investigation with a method you will use right up until the day you select a college. Let's call it T & R, which is short for "talk and read."

Talk to anyone "in the know." As you near the time when the college application process begins, you will speak to your counselors about how they see you and how colleges are likely to view your record. You will find out which colleges they feel should be on your investigation list. You will also speak with your parents to find out what they suggest and how the finances of your education will work.

When you are in the midst of applying, visiting the college and talking to students is another good way to find things out. Most prospective students like to schedule an interview during their visit. The interview gives the admissions people a chance to know you, and gives you a chance to ask questions about the direction and philosophy of the college. But for now, if you'd like some information, speak to any college students you know. Find out what they like and don't like about their schools. These conversations will help you figure out what will be important for you during the college experience.

The counseling office of your high school, the public library, and your local bookstore all have books on colleges. There are books on how to get in, others describing what each school has to offer, and still others, compiled by college students, that tell you what each school is "really like." There are books on Ivy League schools and books on the interview process. You will find almost all of them tremendously useful, though you certainly won't need to read each one cover to cover. There is a lot of repeat information among them.

In addition, individual college catalogs, available through admissions offices (just call or write), make for fun reading and are chock full of detailed information. They describe the college's approach to education, the many academic departments, the student body, admission requirements, the location, the facilities, and anything else you can think of. Catalogs serve as advertising tools for colleges, so they will probably all make the schools sound wonderful. But a careful second reading usually reveals the strengths and weaknesses of a particular college. You will, with the advice of books and other people, be able to tell if you and the school are a good match.

There are thousands of colleges from which to choose, and so your first job will be to narrow down the possibilities. The factors described below should help you do this. They are qualities that affect every aspect of campus life. Of course there is always some amount of compromising you will have to do (no place is absolutely perfect), but if you get most of what you need, you've made a terrific match.

CLOSENESS TO HOME

Everyone's responsibilities and needs are different. Some students may find it necessary to choose a college within commuting distance of their homes. They may need to come home every evening, or stay with relatives and return home every weekend. Perhaps someone at home is ill or disabled, or maybe the family finances simply cannot bear the cost of living on campus.

Fortunately, because there are so many colleges across the country, most students are able to choose a school that is both right for them and close to home.

If you do intend to commute daily, you will want to make sure the school has a comfortable student lounge and library and that inexpensive and safe transportation is available to take you back and forth from home. There will be evenings when you will want to stay late on campus, and while friends may offer to let you sleep over in the dorm, occasionally you may not be able to do so. Safe transportation is critical, so that you can stay on campus as late as you like without fear of returning home in the dark. You might also want to choose a school to which many students commute. It will feel good to help each other out with the typical problems commuting sometimes causes, such as finding places to grab a quick, inexpensive dinner, or sharing notes when one of you misses the first ten minutes of a class because the bus was delayed.

It would be dishonest to say that commuting students have exactly the same college experience as residents do. It is different. Students who commute function within two worlds while those living on campus are totally immersed in one. Things can get rather complicated for students who live at home because they have to juggle many responsibilities and a complex schedule. But this does not in any way mean that commuting students miss out on everything that is fun and exciting at college.

Everything in this book still applies. The classes, the social life, the activities, and more, are all a part of the commuter's life. And the more friends he or she makes, the more comfortable and easy balancing academics, home, and friends will become.

> At first I felt a bit out of it. Everyone seemed to have made friends with the people in their dorm. But then I got friendly with one girl, who invited me back to her room in between two classes. I met two other girls there and when I mentioned it was a little tricky for me, not having a place of my own to relax, all of them said, "Oh! You can use my room!"

The key to enjoying college is leaving yourself open to the experience. You could spend every night in a dorm, but if you're not willing to join in the spirit of the place, you could easily miss what is special about college. In a way, commuters have an advantage. They have no choice. Since they can't hide in a dorm, they spend most of their time right in the thick of things!

SIZE

The size of the college or university you attend is very important. (Universities tend to be bigger than colleges because they include graduate and professional schools and sometimes even several small colleges.) The size has an effect on everything from the number of students and style of classes, to campus facilities (such as sports centers, labs, and libraries), to the amount of academic attention you can expect to receive. Both big and small schools have their advantages and disadvantages.

Small colleges, which may have under a thousand students, offer more personal attention. The ratio of professors to students is low, so that instructors are able to spend more time with their students. Many classes are seminars, with about ten to twenty students, where relaxed conversation and lively debates are encouraged. At Sarah Lawrence, for instance, most classes are limited to fifteen students, and during freshman year each student meets weekly with the teachers. Also, a small college offers a warm sense of community or "family." Everyone knows just about everyone else, creating an environment that is close and supportive.

> I could not believe that two days before exams I got so sick! I had already done a lot of my studying, but I just couldn't get out of bed to take any tests. When I was finally a little better, my friends actually got the professor to let them bring me the exam. On the honor system I took it in front of them. And I did very well!

However, there are drawbacks too. Small colleges cannot offer the kind of student and academic diversity or facilities that larger institutions can. Course selection within certain if not all departments may be limited. For instance, a course on the psychology of the family may not be offered. Instead the psychology department may offer only standard courses such as abnormal psychology and child psychology. The library may contain an unimpressive number of books, and though socially it's nice to discover you know practically everyone, it can begin to feel very restricting by your third year. Some people claim the student body of a small school tends to be uninteresting and "all alike," though others would argue that all kinds of students from all parts of the country enter small colleges . . . it's just that there are fewer of each type.

Large schools with enrollments between fifteen thousand and fifty thousand can offer exciting academic and social options. There tends to be a large, interesting selection of courses in many departments besides the standard offerings. For example, in addition to History of Ancient Greece, the University of California at Santa Cruz offers a more specialized course entitled Ancient Greek Religious Sanctuaries. Libraries tend to be large, with up to 14 million volumes, and sports facilities can be dramatic. Ohio State's Larkins Hall, the main athletic facility, boasts five swimming pools, six gymnasiums, forty racquetball courts, and more. The student communities at large schools are often quite diverse, and social activities on campus are varied.

Large schools can, however, present students with a difficult academic situation. There are many students for every one professor, and so there is less opportunity for help and guidance in planning an academic schedule. It is hard work for students to make themselves known and to ask for what they need. Students who can depend on their own motivation learn the most. Lecture classes with sometimes more than three hundred students, in which the professor delivers a speech while everyone takes notes, are more common than seminars. Short-answer and multiple-choice tests, when the subject matter allows, are more the rule than essays and papers. Also, while students make their own "families" within the busy, large campus, there can be a sense of isolation. The community feeling of smaller colleges is often lacking.

> When I got back to campus from Christmas vacation, I felt a little lost. Most of my friends hadn't returned yet, and everything just seemed so big and empty. . . .

So much for generalizations. The truth is, in almost every case it's important to investigate the facts. Some small colleges have renowned libraries. Hamilton College's total enrollment is under two thousand, but the Burke library houses a sixty-terminal computer center! Some large universities have poorly equipped lab facilities. To learn the truth you have to T & R.

Are you a person who likes to move in big groups, or does a close-knit circle of friends in a cozy atmosphere feel better to you? Are you a person who enjoys small classes, lots of student participation, and close personal contact with teachers, or do you think you'll feel challenged and happy taking in the lessons of a good lecturer? If you can't make up your mind, it may be that you need something in the middle.

There are medium-sized colleges and universities that offer some of the best qualities of both small and large schools. With enrollments of between three thousand and ten thousand students, they are neither overwhelming in size nor too cozy. Also, the course offerings may include equal numbers of lecture and seminar classes so that you can learn in the style you like most.

But be careful. Medium-sized schools can have many of the problems big and small ones do. They may still offer too many lecture classes in an area you'd rather study through seminars, too few courses in certain departments, and a location that is unappealing. In other words, "happy mediums" are not always the answer. For some students a medium-sized school may be perfect. But it won't be just its size that makes it so. It will be that factor combined with all the other elements of college life that make it the "right" place.

LOCATION

City and rural schools have very different things to offer, both positive and negative. Unfortunately, people tend to generalize, confusing the facts. They think that cities are either thrilling and nonstop fun, or frightening, dangerous, lonely, and ugly. They may believe that rural campuses are surrounded by farms and are either beautiful and close-knit or boring and unsophisticated.

In some cases these generalizations will be true, but in others they aren't true at all. Whatever you choose, be aware that location has a big influence on a college experience.

A city college can be an exciting, fast-paced experience. No matter how big or small the city nearby, museums, theater, restaurants, and concerts usually abound, and many students take full advantage of their availability (however, many don't!). Contrary to popular belief, the city campus does have a feeling of community. As in any school, there are student centers, organizations, cafeterias, dorms, libraries, and everything else right "on campus." Columbia University, for example, located on New York City's West Side, has a number of student centers *and* a grassy "quad." The boundaries of the school may be less obvious than those of a country setting, and a new college building may look much like an office building two blocks away, but there is still a campus.

Perhaps one of the biggest physical differences between a city and rural campus, other than the thick trees and meadows, is the relationship between the college and the community. The expression "college town" usually means that the college dominates the town . . . that the town is constantly filled with students eating, seeing movies, shopping, and wandering about. This is common with more rural campuses. But in big cities college students are just a small part of the varied population.

Rural campuses offer a unique, lovely, and often intense experience. Set away from a large city, though often located in or just outside small towns, the college becomes a world unto itself. Students look more to themselves than to bordering communities for entertainment, socializing, and cultural events. The sense of comradeship tends to be very strong as students participate in campus life. Still, because of the relative isolation of a rural campus, some students do feel too closed in. And because of the way the college centers on itself, it can also be very competitive academically. On a city campus, when the pressure gets too intense, students can venture out into the world and "lose" themselves for a few hours. On a rural campus it's more difficult to get away from the tension.

Traditional architecture gives the campus of Kenyon College in Gambier, Ohio, a graceful feeling.

There are many colleges, set in the suburbs near big cities, that appear to be a good compromise for students who want both a rural setting and the excitement of big-city life. But it's important to realize that this setting does not always offer the best of both worlds. That serene country feeling may be missing, despite the trees. And that fast-paced city life is likely to be at least a thirty-minute bus or train ride away. What you do get is relatively pretty and quiet surroundings and a fun urban experience that takes a little planning. For some it's the perfect setup.

If you're a city kid, the lure of studying beside a lake surrounded by trees might be very strong. If you're a country kid, the idea of walking down a busy street teeming with people, interesting places to eat, and a fabulous art store might seem too tempting to resist. But do understand that the lake and the busy street are only part of the picture. They are not the whole experience. And it's the whole experience you are going to have to live with.

PUBLIC OR PRIVATE?

In recent years the cost of attending private colleges has skyrocketed. Public universities are becoming more and more attractive, offering much less expensive tuition and, in most cases, academic departments that are varied and strong. Often these universities have even better-equipped facilities than private schools, and students emerge from the experience with a fine education.

So why bother with a private education? There are a number of reasons. Perhaps you want to major in music and a particular private college has a very strong program with a renowned professor. Maybe you would like to concentrate in a special scientific area and only one or two private colleges near you offer strong departments in that field. In other words, for some it's not a question of choosing to attend a private or public institution. Rather, the decision revolves around what a school can offer, apart from the cost.

There is another reason why some students will opt for a highly rated private college—prestige. A lot of people think it looks good to graduate from a well-known private college or university.

Most public universities do not have the strict admissions requirements that many private schools do. A student attending a highly selective private college can be assured that most of the other students are as well educated and smart as he or she. This is not always so at public universities, although some, like the University of Michigan, are quite selective.

The question is, should that matter? Many people believe the college experience is only complete if you attend classes with a mix of students, instead of just those from one mold. Only then can you enjoy a true exchange of different ideas.

> I wanted to go to school with kids who had all kinds of abilities. Not ones that were the same as mine. That way I would have a chance to hear about other ideas! I tended to be interested in only what I knew I was good at. Meeting other kids who had strengths in other areas opened me up a lot.

Also, in this competitive world, the job market is very tight. People assume that the best jobs go to the graduates of the best schools. In some instances this is quite true. But many people also believe that as you climb the career ladder, what counts is what you have to give. The further you get from that first job, the less the name of your college has to do with your future.

A hard-working graduate from a prestigious private college will always feel a sense of pride and accomplishment. But a hard-working graduate from a state university should feel the same way. Prestige does not necessarily mean the "best" education. A school can't just hand that to you. A student has to work for it.

THE EDUCATIONAL APPROACH

The educational approach of a college plays a significant role in a student's academic experience. It influences the kinds of courses that are offered, the requirements for graduation, fields you can major in, and how courses are taught. But perhaps most importantly, the educational approach affects the campus attitude.

Liberal arts colleges believe students need to open their minds to all the great ideas of the world. The philosophy is to develop each student by broadening his or her sense of the world through the study of literature, history, the arts, and the sciences. Reed College, for example, requires all freshmen to take a course called Humanities 110. Professors from the social science and humanities departments take part, offering students many different perspectives on various subjects. The educators at liberal arts schools are supportive of a student's desire to become a professional in any number of fields, such as medicine or law, and will plan that student's academic schedule accordingly. But for the most part, the school is more concerned with giving students wisdom and knowledge about themselves and the world that can then be used to reach for and achieve goals.

> There's plenty of time for job hunting. When else am I going to get a shot at studying how Greek mythology shows up in the world's great art? It's all so beautiful!

If college means a chance to explore an art form you've always enjoyed, while at the same time studying about a fascinating age in history and a particularly interesting mathematical theory, then a liberal arts education is probably for you. Even if you know specifically what you want to be, such as a doctor, lawyer, or architect, this kind of school can give you a wonderful educational base. You simply need to choose one in which the departments most closely related to your interests are strong. For instance, if you want to be a doctor, then be sure the biology and chemistry departments enjoy good reputations.

However, if you are quite committed to a certain career path and want to concentrate most of your energies there, another slightly different route is available.

More and more colleges are now referring to themselves as *preprofessional*. They are doing so to answer the needs of many students who feel that a liberal arts education does not prepare them well enough for the job demands in the real world. Employers aren't interested, they claim, in a liberal arts degree. In many instances these complaints are valid. Those students with liberal arts degrees who have not gone on to achieve advanced degrees often flounder for a year or two until they either decide to go on to graduate school, or choose a field they are interested in and, starting at the bottom, work their way up. Preprofessional colleges offer academic programs that prepare students for a profession upon graduation. Notre Dame is a good example. It offers strong programs in the College of Science and Engineering and the College of Business. The students who attend are very goal-oriented and many of them plan a study program geared for specific jobs. Of course, these students also usually have to start at the bottom in their professions and work up. A degree from a preprofessional college does not immediately guarantee a vice presidency at a major company! But it will often open doors, and it gives you a very strong base from which to work and learn.

> I'm glad I zeroed in on accounting. The job market was so much easier to get into for me than it was for my friend who majored in European history!

If you want college to lead you directly into a specific high-powered career, then a preprofessional educational approach may be right for you. The experience can be more pressured and smaller in scope than a liberal arts education, but if you are certain of what you want to do, it's something to consider.

SPECIALIZED SCHOOLS

There are some colleges whose programs are designed to meet the needs of students with special talents, skills, or interests. Students sure of their desire to enter the arts, for example, can enroll in institutions that help them develop an extraordinary ability. These schools are usually not labeled preprofessional or liberal arts. They are places for the talented to receive special instruction and attention from leaders in their fields. Rhode Island School of Design, for example, gives students the skills they need to be graphic artists, painters, architects, illustrators, potters, and so on. The Juilliard School offers three departments: music, dance, and drama. Students are required to study the humanities and the history of Western culture, but their concentration is on artistic and technical performance. Most students who attend these specialized schools go on to pursue careers in their chosen fields.

MINORITY SCHOOLS

It is important to consider whether you would like to attend a predominantly white or black school. For black students, there are two ways to look at it. A predominantly white school may better reflect the world you will be entering. The "minority" experience and all the difficult and positive feelings it may cause can be met and dealt with on campus, as a kind of preparation for later on. Also, in terms of the job market, graduates of well-known, predominantly white colleges may get a more favorable hearing. On the other hand, attending a predominantly black school can be a useful opportunity to develop a strong sense of your heritage and place in the world. Lectures, courses, and organizations centering on the black experience, for instance, offer a chance to learn and to draw strength from students with a similar heritage . . . a strength that will help immeasurably after graduation.

It was the smartest decision I ever made. I came away knowing who I am. That I can do it. And that I had an alma mater that gave me a great education and really cared about me even after I graduated!

Morehouse College, one of the foremost private black colleges in the nation, is a demanding school with a list of impressive graduates including Dr. Martin Luther King, Jr. The students emerge confident and prepared for the work world. The ambitious graduates are fond of saying, "You can always tell a Morehouse man, but you can't tell him much."

If you are a minority member who would like to attend a predominantly white school, remember to ask important questions. How big are the minority communities? How many minority members are on the faculty? Are courses offered geared to the minority experience? What are the attitudes of the surrounding town? The degree of social consciousness on campus will be very important for you.

COED OR NOT?

The number of single-sex colleges has declined steadily since the 1960s. Students of opposite sexes seem for the most part to enjoy seeing each other in the classroom. Most students claim it makes studying fun and adds a spirited edge to the natural classroom competition. So why does anyone bother going to a single-sex school? It seems the best answer has to do with camaraderie. All-male schools provide men with an opportunity to support and encourage each other away from the curious eyes of nearby women. And for women, a single-sex school gives students a chance to form a powerful sense of community and a philosophy about their place in the world.

In most instances there is an opposite-sex college nearby, so socializing is relatively easy. If students are motivated, dating and relationships are always possible. The women at Smith College, for instance, date men from Amherst, Hampshire, and the University of Massachusetts.

But most students who attend coed schools feel they've learned a tremendous amount about people of the opposite sex simply by living next door to them. They feel it is an experience that has helped them understand a great deal about friendship and romance.

> I had never had a girl for a friend. I was used to hanging out with the guys. But suddenly I found myself living next door to two really nice women, and I couldn't believe how great it was. I finally figured out they're people too.

WITH OLD FRIENDS AND FAMILY, OR WITHOUT?

Lots of students want to attend college with their good friends or with an older sibling. Somehow it makes the idea of going to college less frightening and more familiar.

But the truth is, going off to college with friends or family is more complicated than it seems. On the positive side, from the day you arrive, college will feel a bit more like home. It's nice to share your fears and excitement with those who know you well. Walking into your first class, attending your first social event, or even just strolling on campus will feel a lot less overwhelming when you're in the company of a good friend. Similarly, knowing that a sister or brother is not far away can give you the confidence to venture out on your own. There's always someone to go to if things don't work out quite the way you planned.

On the down side, attending college with old friends or family can stand in the way of some important experiences. Going to college on your own and fighting a case of nerves is good for you. First, it's excellent practice for real life. After all, you can't bring a friend along to your first job! But more than that, being on your own can force you to find ways to communicate with others and to reach out more wholeheartedly. New relationships will develop more quickly. It's important to remember that you are beginning college on your own but not alone. Everyone will be as anxious to form friendships as you. Part of the college experience is forging new and different relationships. As for family, there's enough competition in college without having to add a touch of sibling rivalry. You may constantly feel as if you have to measure up to a sister's or brother's record. Sometimes it's better to make your own way with your own successes and failures. That way all you have to worry about is you.

Having an old friend or brother or sister nearby can be both comforting and restricting. Whatever you decide, stay aware of the pitfalls. That way you won't fall in!

WHAT IF I HATE WHERE I END UP?

If you hate where you end up, the answer is simple: transfer. Many people do it. In fact, transferring is so common that many colleges have separate transfer applications.

Sometimes, despite all of the reading and all of the talking and all of the investigating, something about the college you attend doesn't feel right. Maybe you thought you'd like to be in a small town, but actually you miss city life. Perhaps you discovered that lecture classes are not your style and that more personal contact would be better for you. It's possible you are troubled by a school's lack of spirit or political awareness on certain issues.

But whatever your reasons, you are in good company. Sometimes it takes spending one year in college to figure out what you want from the remaining three.

So don't worry about making a "mistake." Actually, choosing a college that doesn't feel right is not a mistake. Rather, it is a lesson. You learned what you really want and need. Now you can get on with your education at a college that is right for you. The only thing you have to concern yourself with is "transfer credit." It's important to try and make sure all of the courses you took in one school count toward a degree at the college to which you are transferring. That way you won't have lost any time or money. This can sometimes be a tricky business, but college guidance counselors can be very helpful on such matters.

There are so many colleges to choose from. When it's time to select just a few, the task may seem overwhelming. But the job is actually very manageable. Just ask yourself the right questions and then start talking and reading.

◆ CHAPTER THREE ◆

Does Everyone Get In?

If you want to go to college, you will. There are at least a few schools for every student that are a good match for his or her abilities, talents, interests, personality, goals, circumstances, and finances.

For many students this fact should be easy to believe. After all, they've always known they would go to college. But there are those who may need further convincing.

Many high school juniors and seniors are not encouraged at home to go to college. Money and family problems have made their parents less interested in education and more concerned with making ends meet. Other, often minority students live in areas where the quality of education is not adequate to prepare them properly for a rigorous college program. Surrounded by people who feel trapped or hopeless, these students may feel that they too can go nowhere. As a result, many high school graduates are afraid to give college a try. They lack personal confidence and the support of those around them. Even if they were to get into a college, these students are afraid they might not make it through.

Many colleges are becoming increasingly aware of this problem and are offering solutions. The College of William and Mary, for example, makes an effort to understand the circumstances of an applicant when deciding whether or not to admit him or her. The college also offers special tutorial programs both before and during the college years to help give students the skills they need to complete their degrees.

No matter who you are and where you come from, you may not get into every school you apply to. Few people do. You may not get into your first or second choice. This is not unusual. But if you apply to a group of schools that match your needs and admissions profile, then have no fear. The college experience will be yours.

WHO SAYS YES OR NO?

Before we go on, this is a good time to put your worst nightmares to rest. Lots of students imagine a group of unfeeling strangers impatiently looking over a heap of applications, throwing some in a pile marked YES and others, with a disgusted shake of their heads, in a huge pile marked NO.

Nothing could be further from the truth! The admissions staffs at colleges are made up of very caring and committed people. No application is rejected by just one person. At least two staff members study each application, whether or not the student looks like a good fit. After all of the applications are read through, three piles are usually made. These are marked NO, YES, and MAYBE. The NO pile is checked over one more time, often by the head of admissions, to make sure a student who might fit in well has not been overlooked. The YES pile is put aside to receive acceptance letters later, and then the MAYBE's are placed on the table. A few and sometimes all of the admissions staff members discuss each candidate's qualities. The students are rated on their strengths and weaknesses in different areas. Sometimes if the staff cannot come to a decision they even write to the student asking for more information.

Finally, there is the waiting list. All colleges receive applications from more qualified students than they can accept. When this happens they place some students on a waiting list. These students are as qualified as the students in the YES pile, but for many reasons, such as the number of students already accepted from a particular state, they are not chosen for the first round of acceptances. After the college mails out its acceptance letters, the admissions committee waits to see how many students decide to attend. If enough students turn them down (which is usually the case), they turn to the waiting list.

But at no time does any admissions staff person take a quick look at an application and then shove a "no" letter in the mail. Colleges expect you to take them seriously, because in return they take you seriously.

STACKING THE ODDS IN YOUR FAVOR

We've already discussed narrowing down the long list of colleges that might interest you. Location, size, finances, and educational approach are all important to consider. But now you will have a different job.

A modern building and an ancient tree provide a backdrop for these students' pose. *Photo courtesy of the University of California, Santa Cruz*

Now you will have to think about making those colleges interested in you! Of course if the school is right for you, there should be no problem. But still, there are two things left to do: (1) Figure out which schools will view you as right for them; (2) Work to put your best foot forward.

WHICH ONES WILL SAY YES?

Applying to colleges can be very time-consuming and very expensive. Most colleges charge a fee to process an application. Therefore it's important to choose carefully. This doesn't mean you should only apply to those that will definitely say "yes!" College is a place to challenge yourself, and the challenge begins at application time. If there's a chance you will get in and it's the school you want, you should give it your all. The key is balance. The worst thing you can do is apply to five schools that will obviously take you because you easily satisfy their requirements, or to five schools that probably won't take you because you probably don't satisfy them. What you need is a list of schools that includes one or two where it's unclear if you will be accepted, two or three schools that seem an obvious match, and, for some students, one "easy in" just to be safe.

In order to compose a solid list of these colleges, you will have to take a good hard look at who you are, what you have to offer, what you may look like on a college application, and what that college seems to be looking for. This is not an easy task, so whatever you do, don't go it alone!

SEEK OBJECTIVE OPINIONS

It is very difficult for anyone—child, teenager, or adult—to view himself or herself objectively. All of us have too many insecurities, worries, fears, and fantasies about ourselves to judge accurately how others will see us. For this reason, on occasion, we need to seek the perspective of others.

At the very beginning of this book we spoke of "talk and read." It's critical that you T & R again when narrowing down your list of schools to the ones that are likely to view you favorably. Most counselors suggest limiting the number of applications to five.

Your college adviser at school will be able to give you a good idea of how colleges will view your application. He or she will look over your academic record, extracurricular activities, and community service. You will discuss your strengths and weaknesses, interests, dreams, and personality traits in terms of how they will appear to an admissions staff. Next, your counselors will help you look at the admissions records of various schools:

- How well do students perform on the standard tests given across the country to measure a student's abilities? These tests are known as SATs and ACTs, and colleges release this information every year.
- What rank in their high school class are most freshmen?
- Is the school likely to be interested in a student's artistic talents, sports ability, or leadership qualities, or is it primarily turned on by a powerful academic record?

- Would the college consider your photography portfolio or your articles published in a local newspaper as part of your application?

Just as you have a distinct personality, so do the colleges to which you will apply. The admissions people know the kinds of students they are looking for and will do their best to fill the freshman class accordingly. Your college adviser should know if you're the kind of student in which that particular school would be interested.

Most of the major books on colleges will tell you about the basic requirements of a college. SAT and ACT scores, grade-point averages, and student profiles can usually be found within the page or two allotted to each school. But perhaps a better source of information is the college catalog itself. It will tell you not only about the average scores and grades of incoming freshmen, but also about the kinds of students the school is looking for and the importance it places on different aspects of a student's application. The University of Wisconsin's undergraduate bulletin states, for example:

> Students lacking rank in class or test scores qualifications may be admitted if, on the basis of other factors, they appear to have a reasonable probability of success.

Kenyon College says of its students:

> They are bright, inquisitive, well-informed individuals, people who have marked themselves as achievers, as 'movers and shakers' in their schools and communities . . . many have further demonstrated their talents in pursuits ranging from writing plays to designing computer programs to tracking stock market performance.

PUTTING YOUR BEST FOOT FORWARD

Putting your best foot forward means two things: You have to be the best you can be, and you have to make sure the colleges know of your accomplishments.

When colleges look at your application, they will look at the whole picture. Not just grades. Not just test scores. Not just extracurricular activities and not just community service or hobbies, jobs, or goals. Each and every one of these things plays a part.

Grades:
Your grades are a reflection of how hard you work and how well you grasp the material you have studied. Colleges will look at your grades to see where your strengths and weaknesses lie, paying particular attention to those grades you received from ninth grade on. Of course, they like to see consistently strong grades, but if yours start out on the lower side yet keep improving, they like that too. It shows you're willing to work hard, and that as you matured you began to take your work seriously.

Academic Course Load:
Colleges look for a challenging program that has prepared you for more advanced work, including a number of units in English, mathematics, foreign language, lab science, and social science. In addition they like to see advanced placement, honors, and elective courses in such subjects as psychology or economics or computer sciences. A strong course load helps them view you as ready for the college challenge.

Test Scores:

Colleges do not look at test scores as a measure of your IQ, but rather as one important measure of your ability to do college work. The Scholastic Aptitude Test (SAT) is a two-part examination taken twice, once during your junior year and once at the beginning of your senior year. It is used to measure your verbal and mathematical aptitude. The American College Testing Program (ACT) is a five-part test that measures your achievement in English, math, science, social studies, and history. Colleges usually require one kind of test or the other. They consider your scores, depending on the test, in terms of how you think and reason (under pressure!) and how they match your grades. If you have good grades in English and score well in that area on the tests, then you are obviously a solid English student. However, if your scores are low, it may mean you have strengths in some aspects of English but not all, and the college may seek to learn more about you and your education to clarify. Or your low scores may simply show that you are not a very good test-taker. Many people aren't, so don't panic. There are lots of courses and books available to help you polish your test-taking skills. Most students report that after taking a course, their scores improved tremendously.

> When I took my PSAT tests in my junior year, I was so depressed! I had a total score of 875! I was a good student though, so my adviser suggested I take a course on SATs. I hated the idea, but I knew I had to do something. So for a couple of months I went to the course every Saturday. Finally I took the SATs again. I was so nervous waiting for my scores. When they finally arrived, I didn't think I could look. But I did. I had broken 1100!

Extracurricular Activities:
Colleges like to admit "well-rounded" students. That means they are not looking for students who study, study, study and have no other interests. They want students who can contribute to various areas of college life. Yearbook editors, drama club members, tennis team members, cheerleaders, and members of the student-faculty committee are looked upon positively. These activities prove you are an involved member of your community—that you have interests in working with others and exploring all of your abilities.

Hobbies:
Most people do something in their spare time . . . something that makes them feel peaceful and happy. For some it's painting, for others it's tinkering with electronics, and for still others it's poetry-writing or designing clothes. Colleges like to see this side of you because it indicates your ability to be self-sufficient and creative all on your own.

Community Service:
Community service teaches you about the importance of helping others. It gives you a sense of how much you have to offer and how important it is to look beyond your own needs. Colleges admire community service because it indicates you care about things other than yourself. Colleges hope that their graduates will emerge ready to make changes both in themselves and in the world. Community service indicates that you will be one of those people.

It's one thing to be terrific. It's another thing to let others know. You have two ways of getting everything you have to say across. One is through the application, the other is during an interview. Most admissions people say they tend to put more weight on the application, because students are often too nervous to be themselves in an interview.

Still, there's a lot you can do for yourself in both cases.

The Application

Be neat! Messy applications indicate a person who does not take college or the admissions procedures seriously.

Answer every question as fully as possible. Even if you think being a member of the Social Activities Committee in tenth grade doesn't count, list it anyway. It shows your involvement.

Essay questions are often the most difficult part of an application. The big question students ask themselves is, "What do they really want to hear?" The answer is *you*. They want you to use the essay to express something about yourself. So answer honestly. Make a rough draft first. Plan out your thoughts. Colleges want to know what you care about and how you express yourself and think. And do follow instructions. If an application asks you not to write more than a page, then don't.

Just for fun, take a look at the following essay questions that may appear on college applications:

- Please discuss your feelings about some special interest or achievement that would help us get to know you. Be creative, original, witty or serious, but most of all be yourself!
- Write an essay beginning with the phrase, "I'll never forget the time when . . ."

- Describe a reading experience you have had that left a lasting impression and why.

Finally, send your application in on time. A late application means you can't keep track of time or are a little irresponsible. Colleges will assume your term papers will be late as well!

The Interview

Most admissions people believe they are not seeing the real you at an interview. Students are often quite nervous and so do not present themselves in the best light. Still, there are things you can do before walking into an interview that should make the experience a lot easier:

- Remind yourself that you are here to find out about the college as much as to let it find out about you.
- Remember that the person doing the interview knows you're nervous. He or she just wants to get a sense of who you are.
- Be prepared for open-ended questions like, "Can you tell me something about yourself?" It's fine to ask your interviewer where he or she would like you to start, or simply to start exactly where you would like. But there's no reason to panic.
- Think in advance about answers to other standard questions such as, What do you hope to get out of college? Why do you want to go to this particular college? What departments are you most interested in?
- Bring along anything you'd like your interviewer to see. An art portfolio, architectural sketches,

poems, a radio you built. It doesn't matter what it is as long as it represents some part of you.

- Try to think before you speak. Take your time. It will give you a chance to say what you mean instead of just filling the silence with nervous chatter.

Essay questions and interviews give you a chance to separate yourself from the rest . . . to bring a special personality to your name. Grades won't do that and neither will test scores or lists of hobbies and extracurricular activities. All of these numbers and words will definitely help, but they won't have your "voice." So try as much as possible to let the real you come through. You are your best ally.

WHAT IF THEY SAY NO?

Every college applicant worries that he or she will be rejected by all the colleges applied to. If you are genuinely capable of college work and make an intelligent selection of applications, this is very unlikely to happen. But what of the colleges that do reject you? How are you supposed to take that? With disappointment and confidence.

It is disappointing to be rejected by a college you would have liked to attend, but do keep in mind that college admissions staffs have a huge and difficult job. Not only do they have to sort through thousands of qualified applicants, but they also have to fill the freshman class in a certain way. They want students from different parts of the country. They want students with different interests. They want students with different academic strengths. What this means is that lots of qualified students can get rejected by a college simply because the college is seeking to enroll a balanced class. Perhaps they've already accepted enough students from your area, or with your interests, or with your academic talents. Of course, you may get rejected because you did not quite meet the standards set by the college. But chances are you will have known all along there was a chance of that.

So, in either case, is this so bad? The important thing is you tried. And more than that, you had the confidence you could do the work if they let you in. Which they might still do! You can always try to transfer after freshman year.

So be disappointed you didn't get in, and then confident you will have a wonderful time elsewhere. Once freshman year begins, you'll be too busy to wonder about other schools anyway!

♦ CHAPTER FOUR ♦

Doesn't It Cost a Lot of Money?

College is very expensive. That is the simple truth. But there is enough range in tuition and enough sources of financial aid to make it possible for almost anyone to attend college. With a little determination, you and your parents, together, should be able to manage.

It is a good idea, a year or two before application time, to sit down with your parents and have a talk about finances. This may not be easy. Many adults do not want to discuss their bank accounts or salaries with their children. You may get all the facts, or you may get none. The conversation may inspire your parents to quietly investigate bank loans or talk to investment counselors—or it may not. But no matter how they respond to your questions, it's important to be patient. College will be a heavy financial responsibility for your parents. They may need time to decide what they feel they can handle.

> At first when my parents and I sat down to discuss college costs, I actually think I saw terror in my mother's eyes. Neither she nor my father would tell me what they could

afford. All they could say was that the numbers they were looking at were too high. But then we started going over all the different ways we could get loans and my chances of getting a small scholarship and the costs began to appear less alarming. They began to say things like, "If you earn your pocket money I think maybe we could get you through."

However, no matter how bleak your parents' financial picture looks, don't give up on a particular school because you think it's too expensive. Many students make this mistake and as a result rule out many very selective schools and often all private colleges. While state universities offer a wonderful education, if your preference is a particular private institution, you owe it to yourself to investigate the facts about that school. You might be surprised by the kind of help you are eligible to receive.

This is not to say that if you try hard enough you'll get what you want. Financial aid doesn't work that way. But not trying for help at all won't do a thing for you either. So at least ask questions such as: What kind of academic profile do the students who receive scholarships or loans have? What is their family income? Can I get an athletic scholarship? How many on-campus jobs are generally available? Are off-campus jobs easy to find? What kind of payment schedules can be worked out so that my parents and I have time to pay the tuition?

Of course, all the planning and investigating in the world sometimes can't keep disappointment away. After getting into your favorite school, you may not get the kind of financial aid you feel you need. Colleges will listen to your arguments, and sometimes they will change part of your financial aid package. But rarely, and not by much.

This can feel terrible. You may even wish you had never applied. But most students who have experienced this frustration agree that once they began their freshman year at another college, they forgot everything and just enjoyed themselves.

> I was so proud of myself when I got into Smith, and so excited! But when I found out I just didn't qualify for the help my parents felt we needed, I was crushed. Angrily I enrolled in a good state school instead and spent the summer sulking. Two weeks into my first year at college, I forgot all about Smith. Who cared? My new friends were smart. My classes were great. And I really liked the campus.

I'M SCARED. SHOULD I START SAVING NOW?

You have some time ahead of you before you go to college. During that time there will probably be many important things, big and small, you would like to purchase for yourself. Depending on the finances of your family, and their attitude toward allowances and jobs, you may need to pay for bus fares, clothes, cosmetics, sports equipment, food, gas, and more. Since you will probably not have a lot of time to hold down a job, it is unlikely that before the summer of your graduation from high school you will be able to save up much money.

But this does not mean that those years before college have nothing to do with handling the costs of college. For one thing, learning how to budget your money is very important. Once you're away at school, and busy with academic work, you will have to pay close attention

Lots of work gets done in the computer lab at Wake Forest University in Winston-Salem, North Carolina. *Susan Mullally-Clark*

to what you spend, and where. Most college students are on a tight budget, so it's good to at least start practicing being responsible for money now. How much money do you need for bus fare? What do you spend on snacks? If you want to buy a special article of clothing, where will you have to stop spending money so that you can afford the purchase? Will you have enough left over for afternoon snacks with friends? Get out a piece of paper and see what the figures look like.

Also, these years before college can teach you how to budget your time so that you can hold down a job, do your school work, and play. Most college students learn to find a balance between these three things. If you do have a part-time job, pay special attention to the way you divide up your time. Are you fitting everything in well, or are your grades slipping and your friends feeling totally ignored? If you can work out the kinks now, the transition to college life will be all the easier.

Of course, despite the fact that you won't have had much time to save, colleges will expect you to contribute financially to your education. When colleges figure out how much money they can loan, give, or allow you to work for, they take into account what you and your family will contribute. They believe that if you are mature enough to take on the college experience, then you are mature enough to share in the payment.

Still, right now there is no point worrying about what you can do to pay for college. At this point only good financial planning on your parents' part can realistically have an effect. So do the one thing you can do instead. Learn how to manage your money. Knowing what to do with it is as important as having it.

WHAT DOES FINANCIAL AID MEAN?

Financial aid is the term used to describe any kind of monetary help given to students to help them complete their college education. This help from a college takes three forms: scholarships, loans, and campus jobs. Many students make use of all three. In deciding the amount to give each student, the college looks at the family income, assets (including, for instance, an owned house), grants or scholarships from other sources, and the contribution of the student and his or her family. A sample financial aid package may look something like this:

Total bills (including tuition, room, and board): $16,000.

Scholarship:	$5,400
Loan:	2,500
Job:	1,700
	$9,600

This leaves $6,400 to be paid directly by the student and his or her family.

Financial aid packages can be difficult to work out, but once the numbers are agreed upon, they usually "work."

Scholarships and Grants

Scholarships and grants are both sums of money offered to students that do not have to be repaid. Scholarships are usually given entirely on merit, while grants are offered primarily based on need.

Possibly the best-known scholarship is the National Merit Scholarship Award (NMSA), which is awarded to 16,000 students a year. It is given on the basis of scholastic excellence, not financial need. A student's abilities and obvious commitment to learning are the only things that count.

A number of highly selective universities also offer merit scholarships of their own. Again, financial status is not a factor. Outstanding students are sometimes awarded up to three-fifths of their tuition. For example, Columbia University offers a John Jay National Scholarship Program, which provides monies for gifted young men and women. Wake Forest University offers Reynolds Scholarships to "creative leaders who will affect society in profound ways." Many colleges offer athletic scholarships in different sports including football, basketball, and even golf.

The practice of giving scholarships without regard to financial need has become somewhat controversial. Many selective colleges are now leaning toward offering scholarships only to those students with strong scholastic records who are in need. Some kinds of grants are awarded almost totally on the basis of need to students from lower-income families.

In addition to scholarships offered by individual colleges and universities, there are those offered by national and local organizations, foundations, and corporations. Some are offered on the basis of community service and others on the basis of a response to an essay question. These awards are often intended for a particular kind of student. For example, Rensselaer Polytechnic Institute offers the RCA Scholarship for an upper-class student in electrical engineering or the Union Foundation Scholarship for residents of New Jersey.

Your college counselor should have up-to-date information on the many scholarships and grants that might be available to you. These scholarships can serve the needs of students with very different skills and interests. If you play the cello, speak Polish, plan to enter a medical profession though not as a doctor or nurse, or are of Armenian descent, there may be a scholarship that fits you perfectly!

Most scholarships, however, do not cover the bulk of the costs for four years at college. While they can be helpful, it often falls to the student and his or her family to manage the rest.

Loans

There are many avenues to pursue in order to receive a loan or grant. You can request a Student Aid Report from the U.S. Department of Education, which will let you know if you and your family qualify for any federally funded programs. The possibilities and rules vary from state to state. The financial aid department of any college will provide you with the up-to-date specifics on any state or federal loans that you might apply for.

Below is a list of some programs to give you an idea of how loans work. Again, keep in mind that the guidelines differ from lender to lender, year to year, and state to state.

- As part of their financial-aid packages, many colleges offer low-interest loans. A payment schedule is worked out in advance to suit the family's financial needs. Students can pay back the money over a period of years after graduation.

- The National Direct Student Loan (NDSL), a fund supported by the federal government and by the repayment of earlier loans, is another low-interest loan program. It is administered by the college and is interest-free until six months after graduation. Interest is modest and repayment is made over a period of years.
- The Guaranteed Student Loan (GSL) is made by banks and other commercial lenders. There is a strict schedule of repayment and a limit to the amount lent, but repayment may not have to begin until about six months after graduation.
- Parent Loans for Undergraduate Study (PLUS) are mostly for parents, but they are also available to graduate students and independent undergraduates. Repayment of the amount borrowed plus interest usually begins within a month or two after the loan is received.
- The Supplemental Higher Education Loan Financing Program (SHELF) provides loans to some students whose families do not qualify for other financial aid programs. The loans are for relatively small amounts.

Jobs

Most students these days earn money during their college years. They do so on and off campus, during the school year or over vacations. Holding down a part-time job can go a long way toward taking care of day-to-day expenses.

The student jobs on campus can also be fun. Managing the check-out desk at the library, working the snack bar, sitting at the bookshop cash register, or doing office work can bring you into contact with lots of other students. It can also force you to work out a strict schedule that can keep your work, school, and social life well-balanced and under control!

> At first, trying to get good grades, hold down a part-time job, and see my friends seemed impossible. I just couldn't figure out how I was going to do everything. But then one night, when I just couldn't take all the pressure, I sat down with my notebook and made up a schedule. Then I followed it. The big surprise was how easy it was! Looking back on it, my biggest problem had been my talent for wasting time!

Most on-campus jobs are reserved for students who have qualified for financial aid. The College Work Study Program (CWSP) is a federally funded program that pays student salaries along with contributions from the college. Some jobs are kept available for students who did not qualify for aid but who still have to earn pocket money. Most of these students, however, look for jobs off campus.

All students, no matter what their financial situation, should keep in mind that spending more than fifteen hours a week on a job can cut into academic responsibilities rather severely. It's important to keep priorities straight. A college job is supposed to make college possible, not impossible.

HOW DO I APPLY FOR AID?

In January of your senior year your parents will file a

financial aid form (FAF) with the College Scholarship Service, a division of the College Entrance Examination Board. The College Scholarship Service sends to the colleges you indicate a figure called the Preliminary Estimated Contributions. This figure represents money you and your family can afford, based on the information furnished in the FAF. Some colleges require an application for financial aid in addition to the FAF, so watch for the different deadlines.

Your most important job is helping your parents. We have already discussed how difficult it can sometimes be for parents to allow you to see their finances, but they would probably still welcome turning over much of the "legwork" to you. In fact, for every college you are interested in, you might want to write down on a piece of paper the following pieces of information:

The basic tuition
Room and board expenses
A list of what is required for the FAF
A list of aid packages offered
Percentages of aid offered for different family incomes
Scholarships you may be able to get
Loan programs your parents should look into
Government programs they should investigate
Ways you can earn your pocket money

Also, there are a number of pamphlets and booklets on paying for college. Presenting your parents with a packet of these references along with the above information on particular colleges can only help all of you.

ISN'T NEEDING FINANCIAL AID EMBARRASSING?

Some people estimate that at least 70 percent of students attending private colleges and universities receive financial aid. If all of these students went around hiding their heads, people would be bumping into each other left and right! College is very expensive and few students have parents who can make the full payments up front. In fact, students whose parents are easily able to pay for everything are often embarrassed to admit it!

> A lot of my friends are getting financial aid, and it took me a long time to admit I'm not. I didn't want anyone to think I was spoiled or getting a free ride. Of course I don't *really* think anyone would have been upset. I work hard and everyone knows it. Still, I'm lucky and it embarrassed me.

Confused ideas about financial aid lead to expensive mistakes. Either you won't get the money you deserve, or you'll enroll in a college you don't like just because it costs less. A clear picture can only help you find the way to a good choice.

♦ CHAPTER 5 ♦

Earning the Degree

In high school few decisions are up to you. You are assigned teachers, courses, class sections, and schedules. The only thing you have to worry about is grades. The school administrators do the rest.

This is not so in college. Every college has its own academic requirements for graduation, but how you fill them is up to you. You have a lot of decisions to make. Within certain guidelines you choose the courses you would like to take. You decide on your own major. You decide if you'd like to take lecture or seminar classes. You select the professors with whom you would rather take a course. These and other choices will play a big part in how well you do.

Earning your degree comes down to filling your basic requirements, choosing a good major for you, selecting courses that you will enjoy, and developing good personal study skills. Your education is in your hands.

WHAT ARE THE REQUIREMENTS?

Every college has its own set of academic requirements, and it is up to you, with the help of your adviser, to make sure you meet them all in a way that suits both your talents and your college's rules. Requirements are those courses a college says you must take in order to earn your degree. These requirements come in many different forms.

A college may require that you take specific courses in specific departments, such as English Composition from the English department. It may require that you take a specific number of courses in particular areas of study; for example, you may have to enroll in two natural science courses or one social science course and one fine arts course. Major requirements are the specific courses and the number of courses in one field you must take in order to prove that you have concentrated on a particular subject, which you have chosen as your major. Finally, you may be required to take "electives," which are courses that you elect, or choose, from any academic department. Usually, requirements fall into all four categories.

Some colleges have special requirements that reflect their innovative approach to education. Antioch College, for instance, requires a cycle that alternates class work with three-month periods of full-time work in fields related to college studies.

Every course you take at college counts toward your degree. Every college adds up the credits you have earned differently. Some colleges refer to a year-long course as one unit. Others refer to it as four or eight credits. Others count your credits in hours spent in the classroom. But no matter how your college totals your credits, the amount of courses required or hours spent for a degree are more or less the same across the country.

Confused? You're not alone! Most students take a while to get things straight. To help you see how it works, here is a look at how one school—Wake Forest University—

outlines its requirements for a degree. (This set of requirements could be different by the time you are ready to apply to colleges, so don't forget to T & R.)

One course in English composition

Two courses in a foreign language, one at the intermediate level and one in literature

Two courses in health and sport science

Three courses in each of four divisions: literature and the arts; the natural sciences and mathematics; history, religion and philosophy; and the social and behavioral sciences.

A maximum of 48 credits is allowed toward a major.

144 credits are required for graduation.

What does all this mean? At Wake Forest one semester-course equals four credits, so during your four-year stay you will take approximately thirty-six courses. You cannot take more than twelve courses in your major. Or to look at it another way, only one-third of your course load can concentrate on your major. Wake Forest wants to be sure you study a broad range of subjects.

WHAT IS A MAJOR?

A major is the subject in which a student decides to concentrate his or her studies. It is usually chosen by the end of the sophomore year because students need experience with many academic departments before they can know what they would most like to study.

The choosing of a major is a very significant event in

a college education, though depending on the school it can take on two very different meanings.

If your college is a preprofessional school, then your major is considered the first step to reaching your career goals. If you are an engineering major, you will take some vital courses that prepare you specifically for graduate programs or jobs in that particular field.

If your college has a liberal arts emphasis, a major can serve as a kind of lookout tower, from which you view and then try to understand other fields of study. If you're a history major, you may come to understand economics, literature, and science within that framework. For instance, when you read a book by Charles Dickens, you will better understand, because of your history major, the background of English life he describes. This approach to a major is considered essential because it brings a unified meaning to your education and gives you command over a specific important area of study. Of course, there are some courses quite unrelated to your major that you may take simply because they interest you. (Even though you may choose to major in French, an interesting math course might appeal to you.) These courses can offer you a break from a certain kind of subject matter and get your mind thinking in new and exciting ways. Most students enjoy this sort of variety in their work.

After selecting a major, students meet with an adviser in that department to go over the requirements of their major. During this conversation they may also discuss courses in other departments that might add to the understanding of their chosen major. When appropriate, students may elect to work in the community to enhance their formal education. A psychology major may decide to spend a few hours a week helping at a hospital out-

An art class at Kenyon College gives students a chance to work closely with the professor.

patient clinic. Also, exciting research trips may be advised. An art major may travel to Europe in a college program to see some of the world's greatest art.

No matter what your college's approach to education, however, a major is a student's chance to dig in—to come away from the college experience with a degree of mastery over a subject and to use that knowledge for understanding the world.

HOW DO I SELECT WHICH COURSES TO TAKE?

From the moment freshman year begins, you will be confronted with countless course offerings that pique your curiosity.

> I didn't know what I wanted to major in. I thought maybe economics, so I enrolled in the basic course, plus English composition, and Rocks for Jocks, which was a silly name for a geology course geared for students who aren't great in science. I had to take something like that to complete my natural science requirement. But then I realized I still needed to enroll in one other course. I considered taking a course that would fulfill the fine arts requirement, but then decided to wait on that. Instead I took this really interesting course called Criminal Law. I loved it!

And even after you've chosen your major, requirements and electives can fill you with a spirit of adventure.

> I am a psych major, but at my school you're not allowed to just spend most of your time studying your major, which is

> fine with me. There's so much I learn about people outside of psychology courses! For instance, I took a course called Black American literature. I felt that I learned as much about human struggles in that class as I did in my required psych course!

The question is how and where do you choose?

Every college issues a catalog describing courses. In this book you will find the courses in each department listed with brief descriptions. After you have considered all the available courses, make a list of the ones you are interested in, but don't stop there!

Talk to people. Find out the names of students who have taken the course with each professor. (Many courses are taught during the same semester by two or three different teachers in different time slots.) It's important to find out the style of the different professors so that you can decide which class to enroll in. Some professors may have a lecture style that you would find boring. Others may have a reputation of moving too quickly or not allowing enough student participation. Some professors may have graduate students helping to grade and lead groups within the class while others may not. The approach and personality of the teacher and anyone working with him or her can often have a lot to do with how well you do.

Also, find out the size of the class. Is it a seminar or lecture? Seminars are small classes and allow for lots of student participation. Grades tend to be based on papers or individual projects. Lecture classes can have hundreds of students and rely largely on the prepared speeches of the professors. Individual attention is rarely given to students. Multiple choice or short answer tests are

Students can contribute ideas and ask questions in a sociology class at Wake Forest University. *Susan Mullally-Clark*

common, and if the class is not broken up into groups and guided by graduate students, papers and projects can be rare.

Next, read. See if you can get hold of the course reading list. Do the texts and outside reading assignments look interesting? Are they highly demanding? Are your other courses too heavy for you to take on another big course? You will want to balance your course load. Take a look at the requirements before you sign yourself up.

Choosing courses at college can be lots of fun. What fascinates you? Greek mythology maybe, or Shakespearean sonnets? What questions would you like answered? Perhaps the roots of the conflict in the Middle East puzzle you. Maybe even the theories of Sigmund Freud. Now is the time to satisfy yourself completely.

One final note. Most colleges allow you to enroll in a course and then, after one or two classes, drop it and pick up another. So if you find a course feels absolutely wrong for you—the professor's style doesn't turn you on, the course is more demanding than you'd thought and your schedule can't handle it, or the reading is not as interesting as you'd hoped—don't fret. Just switch.

CAN I STUDY THE SAME WAY I ALWAYS HAVE?

That depends.

Do you set aside time just for studying without the TV or radio blaring? Do you budget your time well so that you don't have to rush to finish your paper or study for a test? Do you know how to study with friends so that you can help each other instead of just socializing? Do you keep up with your assignments daily so that you can absorb the material intelligently, instead of cramming it all in at the last minute, missing important themes and issues? Do you really know how to use the library, as opposed to simply looking one thing up in an encyclopedia? Do you know when you need help with an assignment so that you don't find yourself in trouble only when it's too late?

If so, you're in great shape!

The key to studying in college is organization. Plan your schedule. Know when you are going to work and when you're going to play. Don't just leave it up to the fates! Meet with a few of the students in your class to go over class material. Other students' views can be very enlightening and can help you understand the ideas presented in the class. Don't be afraid to visit your professor if something is confusing you. Just plan to do so before the test, so your grade doesn't "talk" to your professor before you do!

Your professors are not interested in seeing you work from dawn till dusk. But when you do sit down to study, you'll get more accomplished if you do it right. Everyone will be pleased with the results.

HOW DO GRADES WORK?

Different colleges grade their students in different ways. Some use a grade-point system, in which, for example, a grade of "4" is equivalent to an "A," a grade of "3" means a "B," "2" equals a "C," and "1" is a "D."

Other schools use the letter grades (A, B, C, D) without the numbers, while many use a simple pass/fail system.

Then there are schools, such as Sarah Lawrence, that use reports written by teachers and sent to the students twice a year.

Papers, quizzes, mid-term exams, and finals are all considered when professors work out your grade. If you're in a seminar, participation will probably have something to do with your grade, especially if you're borderline between two possible grades.

In fact, when it comes to grading, there are really no surprises. You should be used to the process by the time you arrive at college. The only difference is this: Professors assume you are adult enough to take responsibility for your grades. They will tolerate few excuses for late papers, lack of attendance in class, and poor test results. If you have a problem that is making it impossible for you to meet your responsibilities, you will be expected to work out with your professor an alternative date for a test or an extension for a paper. If you act like an adult, your professors will treat you like one and will make an effort to understand your predicament.

Earning your degree takes maturity, not just grades. What really counts is what you learn, and how you are able to use this knowledge in every aspect of your life. Of course, grades will matter if you intend to go on for a more advanced degree, but even so, it's the quality of the education you allow yourself that will be most important after the classes and grades are all over.

Getting a good grade in psychology does not mean you will make a good psychologist. Knowing the right answers is one thing, understanding how to apply what you've learned is another. As the ancient Greek philosopher Heraclitus said, "Much learning does not teach understanding."

◆ CHAPTER SIX ◆

Roommates

Your roommate is probably the first person with whom you will begin a relationship at college. He or she may not become your closest friend, but for a while you will play a significant part in each other's lives. You will want to treat the relationship with care.

WHO MATCHES US UP?

In most cases colleges do the matchmaking. After you have been admitted, many colleges send either roommate questionnaires or registration forms that include space for stating your preferences about roommates. This is your opportunity to describe the hours you keep, your academic interests, your favorite music, sports you like to play, and so on. Once you send the form back, staff members will try to match you up with someone who seems compatible with you.

Williams College, for instance, regularly sends a room application to incoming freshman. It says,

> Williams seeks to create freshman living units that reflect the variety within each class. Freshman dormitory assign-

> ments are made in an effort to foster the educational experience of living with classmates of different interests and backgrounds. The college also recognizes the need for roommates to be compatible. If you would strongly prefer a particular rooming situation, you may indicate below your requests—for example, particular roommate(s), a nonsmoker, a roommate of your own race, someone with a particular academic or extracurricular interest, someone who will not play loud music, someone who will not stay up late at night, etc.

Of course, you have to realize that a questionnaire is only a piece of paper. What a person seems like on a piece of paper may have very little to do with what he or she is really like. You may get along, or you may not. In any case, you aren't stuck. If the match is truly dreadful, you can apply to switch roommates.

Some colleges will honor your request to room with a friend who is also enrolling at the school. But most will not. They believe you will have plenty of time to spend with your old friend. Assigning you a stranger for a roommate is the school's way of helping you get the most out of the college experience as soon as possible. It will immediately force new experiences into your life.

IS SHARING A ROOM WITH A STRANGER HARD?

Sharing a room with anyone can be a little tricky, especially if you've never done it before. If you've always had your own room, it will be difficult getting used to the fact that you can't just do as you please. You may be used to throwing your clothes all around the room. But if your roommate doesn't like that, you'll have a problem. You may like to listen to music late at night, but if your roommate likes to go to sleep early, you'll either have to buy headphones or go out.

If you have shared a room with a brother or sister, you probably already know what it's like to be considerate of someone else's needs. But even so, you've only become used to one person's habits. Your roommate's will probably be very different.

There is no point worrying about sharing a room with a stranger, because very soon you won't be that to each other at all. What you will be are two people, living together in very close quarters, who should learn to get along.

Here is some basic roommate advice.

Give Your Roommate a Chance

Your roommate may look and act very different from you. He or she may be from another part of the country where the kids don't use the same expressions you do, wear the same kinds of clothes, or even enjoy the same activities. Your roommate's family may have a totally different background from yours, and so she or he has grown up with particular beliefs or attitudes that you can't share.

But no matter what your differences, try to remember that what counts the most is the person inside. He may dress "funny" but he might also be the kind of roommate who would think to bring back food from the cafeteria when you're not feeling well. She may think your socializing style is kind of wild, but she may be there for you if one night you end up crying over a broken romance.

Of course, it's always wonderful when two people shar-

Students take time out for a chat on the campus of Wake Forest University. *Bill Ray III*

ing a room have so much in common that they also become close friends. Then late night conversations can be great fun. But freshman year you just can't count on it. What you can count on, however, is having a real human being for a roommate . . . as long as you treat him or her like one.

Don't let your differences stop you from seeing the person inside. If you can respect each other's style, your freshman year should at least be peaceful.

Decorate for the Two of You

Your room at college will be your private spot to dream, work, and enjoy some friendly socializing. You will want it to reflect your personality. The problem is, your roommate will feel the same way. If you are very different people, you will have a lot of compromising to do.

Some roommates write to each other during the summer before college begins and decide on a color scheme. They may each buy the same color bedspreads or small rugs to throw on the floor. But lots of roommates don't bother with this. They arrive at school, meet their roommates, and immediately start discussing what they need to make the room look nice and feel comfortable.

When you have these discussions, remember to be aware of:

The Expense:

Your roommate may not be able to afford all the purchases you are intending to make. Conversely you may not be able to afford what your roommate would like. Make sure the conversation stays frank and open. There's nothing to be ashamed of either way.

Personal Style:

You may like bright, intense colors. Your roommate may feel much more comfortable with darker, subtle shades. There's no point arguing or trying to convince the other that a particular color is really better. It's a matter of taste. The solution may be to pick an intense and a subtle color that blend together nicely.

Interests:

Your different tastes in music and art or involvement in sports or politics will usually find a way into room decoration. You may want to plaster your side of the room with pop singer posters and your roommate may want to hang up prints of Italian Renaissance art. The two just don't go together. But one thing is for sure. Neither one of you should give in entirely to the other's preferences. The only thing you should do is let go of your fantasy college room. The room may not end up being color-coordinated with prettily arranged pictures, or have all four walls filled with portraits of today's biggest sports stars. But that doesn't mean it will look awful or lack personality. It may in fact look twice as good, double-loaded with personality!

> I'll never forget walking into my room for the first time armed with Broadway theater posters to fill the empty walls. Instead, I found my new roommate standing on a chair fastening a giant poster of Mick Jagger next to the one she'd put up of Tina Turner. I thought to myself, "Oh boy, am I in trouble." I put my posters in the closet. But a week later she asked me, "Don't you want to put anything up?" I mumbled something about our things not going together, and she said, "So what! Let's see!"

> So I showed her. She thought my posters were gorgeous and even took down one of hers to make room for a particularly big one of mine. I began to think Tina Turner wasn't half bad.

Your room will always be a reflection, at least in part, of who you are. And that's only fair. You can't really expect more. After all, it has to do the same for your roommate.

Coordinate Your Schedules

Some people call themselves "night people," some "morning people," and still others "afternoon people." They all feel they are especially productive during certain times of the day.

If your roommate's personal schedule is very different from yours, it can pose problems for you, and vice versa. For instance, perhaps your roommate feels he does his best work early in the morning, and so he wants to turn the lights on earlier than you would like. Since you tend to do your best thinking in the afternoon, you need that extra hour of sleep in the morning. Or maybe you'd like to see your friends late at night. That's when you feel relaxed. The only problem is, that's when your roommate wants to go to sleep.

It's clear each of you has to compromise a little bit. If your roommate wants to read in the morning, there's nothing wrong with asking him to do so in the dorm lounge or in the library. If you want to party late at night with your friends, you can do so in someone else's room or in the student center. Of course, both of you will need to be a little flexible. Your roommate will have to turn on some lights in order to get dressed in the morning. And there's nothing wrong with occasionally having a few friends come for a late visit in your room . . . as long as your roommate doesn't have a big test early the next morning!

The only way to coordinate your schedules is to keep your eyes open and keep talking. If your roommate likes to bring friends back to the room after class right at the time that you settle down to get some work done, don't just regularly pack up your things and leave. There are plenty of places for him to socialize. The first time it happens, relax, and when his friends leave, explain how you feel.

> I had just settled down to get some work done when my roommate walked in with two friends. Quietly I packed up my stuff and went to the library. The next day the same thing happened. Again I snuck away. Finally I couldn't stand it anymore. Not that the library wasn't nice. I just liked to work in the room. So I said, "Look, Jim, I really like working in the room in the afternoon. Can you sometimes meet Mike and Paul somewhere else?" Much to my surprise, he just laughed and said, "Sure! This room's too small for all of us anyway!"

DO I HAVE TO HAVE THE SAME ROOMMATE AND ROOM ALL FOUR YEARS?

Absolutely not! Freshman year you are assigned a roommate, largely because you are in no position to choose one and colleges prefer you share with someone new. But after that it's up to you. At the end of freshman year, most students make arrangements to share with a friend or friends, and all they have to do is inform the housing office.

Which brings up another point. Some colleges have enough dorm space to house everyone. There are single rooms, double rooms, and even small suites where three or four rooms open up onto a common living space. You can usually apply for any of these situations. However, some schools simply do not have the room to house everyone. In these cases students venture out into the town and find small apartments or sometimes entire houses to rent with other students. This can be a great deal of fun. There's a kitchen, more privacy, and a greater feeling of independence.

Living off campus in this way is not advisable freshman year, because the first year is your opportunity to get to know your campus and as many people on it as possible. Obviously the best way to do this is to live right in the center of all the action!

What it gets down to freshman year is this. Your first roommate is usually chosen for you. You may like the choice, or you may not—there are no guarantees. But certainly there is bound to be enough about this person to respect and appreciate. You may not end up being the closest friends, but if you can keep these three things in mind, the year should go smoothly: You don't have to love people to get along with them; people who are different from you can open you up to exciting new experiences if you let them; your roommate is a person you share your room with, not your life.

So don't panic. There are lots of people on campus with whom to make friends. Some students report, in fact, that it's better not to share a room with your closest friend. Sometimes, when there are a lot of important feelings between two people, it's harder to set rules. People's sensitivities get in the way. An honest, fair person, whether or not he or she has much in common with you, may be your best bet after all!

♦ CHAPTER 7 ♦

Socializing on Campus

When I first heard about coed dorms, I thought "*Wow!* Girls everywhere! Maybe even right next door! No parents anywhere!" But then I got to school, and boy, was I surprised. The girls who lived right near me ended up being incredibly great friends to me. Like family. And the biggest surprise of all was I liked it just that way.

SOCIAL LIFE/DORM LIFE

Just the idea of dorm life can seem incredibly exciting. There you are, away from home, surrounded by kids day in and day out, deciding your own hours, studying when you please, hanging out with whomever you like, as late as you would like. Romance at every turn. What could be better?

Well, it is a fun experience, but of course nothing is ever exactly as you imagine it. Here is how dorm life works.

Single-Sex Dorms

In terms of day-to-day living, when a dorm is occupied by only one sex, things are particularly relaxed. People wander up and down the hall in nightgowns or pajamas, or underwear and T-shirts, with barely a second thought (though most students advise taking a quick peek down the hall in case someone has an opposite-sex visitor!). Once students have been in the dorm for about a month, they even relax their behavior in bathrooms. Self-consciousness goes out the window.

Socially, an all-female or all-male dorm can feel much like a sorority or fraternity. Close friendships form on the hallways. Friends either get together in their rooms, or in student lounges in the dorms. These friends often walk to the library together, eat together in the cafeterias, attend dances and concerts together, and generally act as a family.

> At first I thought, "I'm so lucky! Right on my own hallway I made two fantastic friends. We have so much in common." But then I looked around and noticed that a lot of people made particularly good friends on their hallways too. It couldn't just be a coincidence. I guess when you live very closely with a lot of people, there will always be a few you can really make a meaningful connection with. Had I lived on another hall, I'd have probably found two other terrific friends!

Coed Dorms

Coed dorms have opposite-sex students on alternating floors, rooms, or hallways. (Bathrooms are usually separate.) Surprisingly, things are usually quite relaxed here too, but not quite as much as in single-sex dorms. Students can still be seen wandering around the hallways in bathrobes, pajamas, and nightgowns, but most admit they take a little extra care before emerging from their rooms.

> After I took a shower, I'd run back to the room, comb my hair out, put on just a little bit of makeup, retie my fluffy pink bathrobe, and only then would I venture out into one of the lounges. Believe it or not, it took me a while to let the guys see me with my wet hair up in a towel!

One of the nicest things about coed dorms is the kind of friendships that emerge between the two sexes. Most students report they feel very much like brothers and sisters, but with one difference—they tend to treat each other better! If most of your friends are having a romance and you are not, there are plenty of opposite-sex friends with whom to spend time. If you are having a problematic romance, it's easy to ask friends for the male or female perspective in a relaxed and cozy atmosphere. Coed dorms provide you with a kind of built-in social life.

Dorm Romance

Of course, students also do form romantic relationships with other people in their dorms. While most students report it rarely happens with the girl or guy next door, it can happen that way, or with someone two floors down or two halls to your left. This, of course, has its positive and negative sides. It's fun to be involved with someone who lives under the same roof. You can get together easily and quickly. You can leave each other notes on your doors. You can walk together to and from classes or the library. On the negative side, it can be a little stifling. You will run into each other a lot, and so it is hard to keep any parts of your lives separate. If one of you would like to simply do something without informing the other, for whatever reason, it could be almost impossible. Too many people who live in the dorm with both of you will know your business.

This points up a basic issue about romance at college, no matter where the two of you live—things can get very intense.

Because a college community or group of friends tends to be close, it's difficult to get any "space." Most romances involve periods of getting very close, moving back a little, taking another step forward, and so forth. To do this, people need to "breathe." They need to go off with their own friends, perhaps try dates with other people, maybe go away for a weekend, or simply spend one day without speaking to their partner. But even on large campuses people often run into each other at least once a day. So students have to make a real effort to understand each other's need for independence.

> Jenny and I got involved the first week of school. We met in our Psych 1 class. We liked each other a huge amount immediately, but after we were going out for about a month, I started to wonder if maybe we'd gotten involved too fast. It wasn't that I didn't like her. It was just that I got, well, itchy. The thing is, it was hard to step back. Even if we broke up I'd see her every other day in class. So I didn't say anything, and instead just started acting a little distant. We started fighting a lot and finally we broke up. Looking back on it, I didn't handle things very well. It was dumb. I missed her a lot.

Socializing in college is not as simple as it seems!

WHAT ABOUT SORORITIES AND FRATERNITIES?

Sororities and fraternities can be, for some students, a tempting world. Some colleges have them and some don't. Sororities and fraternities offer a strong sense of belonging to a small, close-knit group of people. They open up opportunities for lifelong friendships, a comfortable social life, spirited sports events, and more. The frat or sorority house can feel like a cozy, self-sufficient, little world where members live, eat, study, and have fun together. They also make decisions together related to house rules, house parties, and community service. Often the fraternity or sorority houses are located next to each other, and most of them hang a flag or banner outside proclaiming the name of their organization.

There is another thing about sororities and fraternities that is not always talked about but is certainly felt: tradition. Often student members have fathers, mothers, or siblings who joined the same organizations at the same school or at a different one. (Most fraternities and sororities are national, so that chapters of the same organization exist across the country.) A sense of carrying on the family tradition brings some students a great deal of good feeling.

However, if you are not following in anyone's footsteps, do not fear. There is usually enough diversity among the different sororities and fraternities, in terms of interests, goals, and heritage, to find the one that is right for you.

Of course, there is still the issue of getting into these organizations. It may be comforting once you belong, but many students resist the temptation to join because the process for getting accepted as a member can sometimes feel judgmental and unfriendly. Though many colleges are now doing away with the snobbish and sometimes even cruel aspects of this process, there remains on many campuses some degree of unpleasantness. First, new students are invited to attend open houses at one or more fraternities or sororities. These occasions are designed to give members a chance to get to know the new students. Sometime later the members vote on which of these students they would like to have join their organization. Then comes the part everyone hears about. Before any new students can officially join, they often have to carry out some unusual orders thought up by the members. Sometimes these orders are funny, sometimes not.

Sororities and fraternities carry varying degrees of importance on campus, depending on the school. If you are not attracted to these kinds of organizations, you may prefer to choose a school that offers many other housing options and many other well-developed social arenas.

GOOD TIMES ON CAMPUS

Most college campuses offer many places and situations for student socializing.

Student Center:

A student center, depending on the size of the campus, can offer anything from just a few large, comfortable rooms with snack machines, couches, chairs, and a television set to, in the case of George Washington University's Marvin Student Center, a plush cafeteria, bowling alleys, disco, and more. These centers are places for students to meet friends, relax, have informal study sessions, and just hang out. They are especially useful for those students who live at home.

Cafeterias:

During breakfast, lunch, and dinner hours the cafeteria is filled with friends enjoying food and conversation. Some cafeterias stay open until early in the morning. After dinner hours they serve as a kind of snack bar, conversation corner, and informal study hall. Students drop in after a few hours of intensive study in the library to joke around and unwind. Others take a seat simply to people-watch.

Library Lounges:

Students often like to step away from their books just for a ten-minute break, and many libraries provide a room where they can chat with a few friends and clear their heads a little. Soda and snack machines line the walls, and students have a chance to make plans for the weekend or even for later that night.

Dorm Parties:

Frequently, students from a particular dorm throw a party. The parties are advertised around campus with handwritten or photocopied signs, and everyone is welcome. Often these parties have themes, like the Roaring Twenties, the Fifties, or California Beaches. Students often dress to suit the theme, and sometimes decorations and food fit in as well. Homecoming week, Halloween, and Valentine's Day are usually celebrated at weekend parties.

Campus Parties:

Some colleges have a few dances each year, held at the gym or in the cafeteria. Live bands may perform, or the music may be provided by records, and a small admission fee is charged. Some colleges have traditional parties. Kalamazoo College in Michigan has a campus-wide dance every quarter, including the winter Monte Carlo Night, which is a formal dance with a pretend casino. Students at every college may attend campus parties with dates, with groups of friends, or all alone. It's a wonderful way to meet new people, or just to enjoy yourself with someone you already know.

On-Campus Movies:

There is usually some form of movie theater on campus, whether it's a real one or simply a large screen unfurled in the gym. Usually organized by a student film society, old movies, classic movies, and movies that have an almost cultlike following are shown. Movie schedules are usually posted around campus, and students often use the evenings on which films are shown as dates. Students have to venture off campus for current hits.

Concerts and Plays:

Rock, jazz, and classical music concerts as well as plays and musicals may all be planned by students on campus and provide an exciting and spirited backdrop for socializing. At smaller colleges such as Bard, student poetry and fiction readings are a favorite pastime.

The Campus Itself:

City, surburban, and rural colleges all have campuses

Students gather to find old friends and make new ones on the University of Michigan campus.

across which most students walk to get from building to building. On a beautiful day these areas are usually filled with kids taking in the sun between classes. Sprawled on the lawn, sitting on benches, or throwing a Frisbee or football around, students gather to spend some relaxed time before they return to their studies.

> I met my closest friend outside of the English Department building. It happened like this: I was a few minutes early for class, so I threw myself down on the grass and started reading the campus newspaper. The next thing I know I hear a voice say, "How 'bout it? We need another guy for baseball at five o'clock. You game?" I nodded quickly, all of us had a great time, and Lou and I have been buddies ever since.

It is very difficult *not* to have a social life at college. There are too many people around with whom to talk, study, and have fun. If you're a shy person, it may take you a little longer to warm up to people. If you're a gregarious social type, you may find yourself changing friends at the beginning quite a lot. (Since relationships at college can get very intense very quickly, you may find the people you first hang out with are not quite your type.) But no matter how your friendships form, you will develop strong, meaningful bonds at school. Of course, no one can escape feelings of loneliness entirely, not even at college where there are students everywhere. But campus is so active, chances are you won't feel alone for too long. There are too many people to meet. Too many places to go. And certainly lots and lots of things to do!

◆ CHAPTER 8 ◆

How About Activities?

Campus activities are as important to the college experience as academic classes. True, they do not count toward your degree, but they do count for *you*. Involvement in campus activities gives you a chance to develop leadership abilities, meet people with similar interests, learn new skills, appreciate other cultures, and feel a part of something special. Whether you decide to stage-manage a show, become the layout editor for the yearbook, learn how to develop your own photographs, march in the student band, join a choir, or go out for the tennis team, there is a campus activity that is right for you.

All you have to do is find it, participate, and cooperate. If you join a games club or a chorus, you will be able to start right in playing Dungeons and Dragons or singing with the other members. But if you decide to work on the campus paper, you might have to wait and learn before you will be allowed to write the concert and play reviews. Someone else with more experience may already be doing that. (When he or she leaves the position, or graduates, it will be your turn.)

Student activities exist on campus because the students make them happen. They are designed to meet your interests. So get involved! It's the best way of making sure the activity will continue. Here is a look at the kinds of organizations you might like to join.

STUDENT GOVERNMENT

Students are usually represented at all levels of college or university governance. Their chief responsibilities are to act on student concerns and make recommendations to the university's faculty community. Student governments are organized differently in different schools, but in general students are elected to the higher positions. Student senates and student/faculty committees deal with social and academic matters, supporting activities that benefit the school and the larger community. Antioch's administrative council, Adcil, is composed of five students, three faculty members, and two administrators. Its opinion has had a powerful influence on such matters as faculty hiring, new programs, and allocation of funds to various aspects of campus life. In other schools student councils have participated in everything from defining a college's policy on alcohol to planning housing lotteries. Finally, honor councils made up of students receive and investigate all charges of violations of the student codes.

Becoming a part of student government will not only exercise your leadership skills, but also allow you to influence critical aspects of the college experience.

COMMUNICATIONS

If you're interested in media, there are lots of organizations or groups to choose from. A campus radio club gives

Film-making lets students exercise their creative talents at Wesleyan University. *Nancy Walz/Wesleyan University*

members a chance to learn and experiment with radio operations. An official radio station of a college presents material students want to hear. Jazz festivals, classical marathons, or special, new, live broadcasts can be heard late into the evening. It's your chance to taste broadcast journalism and DJ fun! At Kenyon College, for instance, a number of students and faculty members have developed and hosted their own shows, including a program that concentrates on music written and performed by women. Students can be disc jockeys, engineers, and members of the business and promotion staffs. Some larger universities also have student-run television stations. This is a wonderful place for students to learn the skills of television production and administration.

In print journalism there are both daily and weekly student newspapers. Some colleges offer liberal and conservative monthly papers that deal with current issues both on campus and off. There are yearbooks and campus magazines that give students a chance to work on photography, layout, design, and editing.

Columbia University, for example, has a broad range of student publications, including:

- *The Asian Journal*—an annual publication that aims to create a greater understanding of Asian heritage and culture.
- *Black Heights*—a literary and cultural magazine that offers a special place for minority students to use their talents.
- *Columbian*—the yearbook of Columbia College.
- *Course Guide*—a publication that attempts to answer students' questions about specific courses and professors in advance of registering.

- *Jester of Columbia*—an official humor magazine specializing in parodies of popular magazines and books.
- *The Columbia Review*—the official literary magazine of Columbia University, which publishes student writings.
- *The Columbia Daily Spectator*—a daily newspaper covering campus and related city and national news.
- *Broadway*—a biweekly magazine on the arts.
- *Upstart*—the annual arts journal of Columbia and Barnard Colleges, publishing student artwork, poetry, prose, criticism, and interviews.

PERFORMING ARTS

Most colleges have a number of theater groups. Some of these are closely tied to the drama department, and others spring totally from the interests and energy of the students. Whether you are interested in Shakespeare, Ionesco, or Wilder, there will be any number of productions you can try out for, work on backstage, or simply enjoy! And if musical theater is your special passion, chances are you will have a chance to explore that world as well. Tufts University's Torn Ticket group has staged *Fiddler on the Roof, A Little Night Music, Guys and Dolls, A Funny Thing Happened on the Way to the Forum, Follies, Cabaret,* and other popular shows.

When it comes to music, you can probably take your pick. Below is a list of musical groups Tufts University encourages its students to join:

Tufts Community Orchestra, Tufts Wind Ensemble, Jumbo Marching Band, Tufts Jazz Ensemble, Tufts Jazz

Band, Early Music Ensemble, Chamber Music Group, West African Drum Ensemble, Tufts University Chorale, Madrigal Choir, Beelzebubs and Jackson Jills (men's and women's singing ensembles), and Amalgamates (a male and female *a cappella* singing group).

Of course, some schools may not have as diverse a selection, while others may offer still more possibilities. The University of Denver, for instance, has the Opera Theatre, which enjoys lots of student participation. If you have a particular performance interest and can find other students with the same ideas, you can form a group of your own and, after bringing it before the college authorities, watch it become official!

ETHNIC

Student organizations based on a particular cultural heritage are common. These groups are formed to give students a chance to foster friendship and a sense of unity. Dedicated to promoting awareness of their communities both here and abroad, these organizations often hold cultural shows, movies, dinners, lectures, and conferences on a variety of interesting and meaningful subjects.

SPORTS

Before you throw yourself onto the field, you have to decide how seriously you want to take athletics at college. If you choose to try out for a team that competes with other colleges, you will experience lots of fun and lots of pressure. Many colleges feel they have reputations to uphold. They may claim to have the best football team in the Midwest or the strongest basketball team in the East. If you're an athelete who thrives on high expectations and performance pressure, then go for it.

The University of Wisconsin, for instance, is a member of the Big Ten Conference and the National Collegiate Athletic Association. It competes in thirteen sports for men—baseball, basketball, crew, cross-country/track, fencing, football, golf, gymnastics, hockey, soccer, swimming, tennis, wrestling—and ten sports for women—basketball, crew, cross-country/track, fencing, golf, gymnastics, soccer, swimming, tennis, volleyball.

But if you like your games just for fun, filled with good humor and with just a healthy edge of competitiveness, then recreational, intramural sports are right for you. You even have a bigger selection to choose from. Wisconsin offers these recreational sports programs to give students relaxation, a sense of belonging and achieving, and most of all, fun: aikido, badminton, boxing, fencing, Frisbee, women's ice hockey, Japanese karate, judo, kendo, lacrosse, rugby, women's rugby, shorin-ryu karate, skating, squash, synchronized swimming, tae kwon do, team handball, volleyball, and water polo.

Every college has its special offerings. The University of California at Santa Cruz offers recreational activities such as mountaineering, parachuting, surfing, and yoga. The University of Iowa has its very own golf course!

RELIGIOUS

Many campuses have student organizations with a religious affiliation. These groups exist to help students further understand the meaning of their faith, to give them a place to celebrate holidays and seek counseling, and to provide community service. Rensselaer, for example, houses the Rensselaer Christian Community, the Rensselaer Newman Student Association, Hillel, and the Islamic Student Organization. All of these organizations involve students in regular meetings, lecture series, and more.

OTHER

Preprofessional groups on campus are formed by students with similar goals so that they can share their knowledge and time with each other. Premedical, prelaw, and business societies are springing up to help those students with focused plans to organize lectures, study groups, and forums. The University of Michigan, for instance, has an Architecture Students Association and an American Student Dental Association.

Women's groups on campus give women a place to air their particular concerns, develop a strong sense of unity with each other, and assure that campus activities and courses reflect their place in the world.

SPECIAL INTERESTS

Are you interested in learning to play bridge? How about taking beautiful photographs? Debating? Maybe chess or Monopoly is your thing? Of course, there is always juggling! Here is a description of a very specialized club at Columbia University that once appeared in their pamphlets:

Amaze friends and family alike by learning to juggle with scarves, balls, even eggs! Join the Columbia Juggling Club, a talented and energetic campus organization that juggles indoors and out (weather permitting). No experience is necessary, so feel free to attend regular meetings!

College is about learning, but not just in classrooms. Participating in sports, government, theater, journalism, or even juggling will teach you a tremendous amount about yourself and other people. So don't take this aspect of college life too lightly. You'll be missing a lot of fun.

◆ CHAPTER 9 ◆

Living Outside Your Family: It's Up to You

When you're living at home, most rules are not your own. Sometimes this fact is obvious and sometimes you can barely feel it. For instance, if your parents want you home by a certain hour, you have to check your watch and be on your way in time to meet your curfew. However, the fact that your laundry is done once a week or that you can expect a big dinner at 6:30 seems to be "just the way things are."

But once you arrive at college those kinds of rules and givens are gone. Of course, every college does have a set of rules it expects students to abide by. But these are mostly concerned with very critical matters. They have to do with things like drugs, drinking, stealing, cheating on exams, plagiarizing, and cutting classes. The official college handbook usually states very clearly the rules regarding these issues, along with the consequences should students choose to ignore the rules. Both the authorities on campus and fellow students consider the guidelines for student behavior supremely important. College communities rely on a certain sense of trust. For this reason it is not uncommon for professors or students to turn someone in who is behaving dishonestly or very irresponsibly. But the bottom line is that as a college student you need to take responsibility for yourself. Within a certain framework it's time for you to decide the way in which you will live. This can be exciting, fun, and interesting . . . but also frightening.

What time should you get up or go to sleep? What do you really think of that girl down the hall who everyone makes fun of? Should you become intimate with someone, even though you think things are moving too fast? How sick should you feel before you visit the infirmary? When should you decide it's time to talk to your professor because of sagging grades? If you bring just a page or two of notes to a test, is that really *so* bad? And perhaps most importantly, when is it time to seek help from advisers or counselors?

The answers? They are up to you. Many of these issues will take a lot of thought and experimenting before you establish what feels right for you. But you needn't muddle through on your own. Here's a look at the support systems available on campus to give you a hand.

Health Care:

Every college has an infirmary open twenty-four hours a day. Nurses are available around the clock, doctors are in attendance daily, and the advice of specialists can always be secured. Medical services such as medicine, routine injections and immunizations, X rays, and laboratory tests are readily available either at the infirmary or the nearest clinic or hospital associated with the college. You can assume most visits are completely confidential, though you have to expect to run into students you know at the infirmary. Minor ailments are generally not reported to parents, but information about anything of a serious nature will be communicated to your home as soon as possible.

Counseling Center:

You will probably experience various problems during your years at college. This is not necessarily a bad thing. One can learn a lot from working through a serious disappointment, frustration, hurt, anxiety, or sadness. Professionally trained and experienced counselors are available to you with complete confidentiality. Some colleges offer individual, group, and couples counseling, while others offer regular groups with a specific focus. Antioch College, for example, has a "Transition to College" group for all incoming students. It is designed to provide support as students cope with being separated from home, family, and friends and try to immerse themselves in the college experience. Many colleges also provide counseling through the chaplain's office or religious organizations on campus.

Academic Counseling:

There are many different places you can go for academic counseling. Your choice depends on your needs and the way your college has set up counseling services. Certainly you can go to the adviser who has been assigned to you, in order to get basic advice as you arrange your course schedule. Often you are also assigned an upperclassman who assists you with any problems. Some colleges have programs like Tufts University's Academic Resource Center, which offers instruction on

Talking with a professor can often help students make decisions about courses. *Shana Sureck/Wesleyan University*

study skills, as well as tutoring from other students in specific courses. Still others, such as the University of Wisconsin, offer group workshops in reducing test anxiety and other, related areas. Finally, you can almost always seek the advice and help of a favorite professor whether or not he or she is assigned to you.

Most colleges also offer specialized counseling for women, handicapped students, and foreign students, as well as help with issues of health, sexuality, and careers. If you have a problem, there will almost always be someone to help you sort it out. But again, the answers and the many choices you will have to make during the college years are up to you.

You can see that you will not be alone. You will, however, be on your own. Only you can seek help and only you will be responsible for your actions.

This is so in many important areas.

THE HONOR CODE

Most colleges have some form of honor code. It exists in order to encourage students to behave honestly. In essence it means that each student's word can be trusted, and that any violation is an offense against the whole community. It charges students with the responsibility neither to give nor to receive help during any exam or quiz, not to plagiarize, to respect other people's property, to refrain from making false statements to any member of the university community, and to insist that any student who does violate the honor system report himself.

As a college student you are expected to treat the experience as a privilege. You do not cheat, because it is a privilege to learn. You treat other students as you would want to be treated, and you recognize it is a privilege to work beside these students, as it is for them to strive beside you.

RELATIONSHIPS

At college there is no one in authority to tell you who to be friends with, who might be a bad influence, and how involved you should get in a romance. You will have to draw on your own values, your past experiences, and the advice of friends and perhaps college counselors to help you handle the difficult demands some friendships and some romances may make upon you. It's up to you to choose friends, avoid certain "crowds," and decide how far you want an intimate relationship to go.

ACADEMICS

We've already discussed where to go when deciding on a major or designing a course load. But what about other issues? What if you think that your grade is unfair, or that your chosen major is not as interesting as you thought it would be, or that in order to write a special term paper you need to take an extra week and do some research off campus? It's up to you. Only you can discuss the grade with your professor, work out a new major with your adviser, or request that extra week from a dean.

DAILY LIFE

The moment you reach college you're in charge of your every move. Do you feel like skipping a class? Studying late at night instead of during the afternoon? Maybe you would like to put off a reading assignment and instead go away for a weekend. At home your parents always insisted you eat breakfast. Would you like to have nothing but a cup of tea now? You've always hated making your bed. Perhaps you'll leave yours a mess every morning now that no one is around to complain.

And then of course there is the matter of your daily schedule. As school begins you will have an entire schedule to plan. A semester full of days to fill! What will that be like? To give you an idea of how a day at college might unfold, here is a page of the diary kept by Alissa, a freshman thinking about majoring in European history.

7:30 A.M.: The alarm woke me up. My roommate was already gone. Threw myself into a pair of jeans and a sweater and ran to the cafeteria for some yogurt. No one there I'm all that friendly with so ate fast and strolled to class.

8:15 A.M.: Basic Astronomy. A lecture. Took notes furiously for 50 minutes. Scared to miss anything that could be on the test coming up in two weeks. Science is not my thing.

9:15 A.M.: Italian Renaissance History. A seminar. Didn't add much to the discussion about the Medici family's contribution to the arts because forgot to read my assignment last night. Felt uncomfortable in class. An hour and a half is a long time to sit with nothing to say in a class so small.

11:00–11:30 A.M.: Went to the library. Did some research for the paper that's due on Italian Renaissance Sculpture. Couldn't find everything I need. May need to take a bus into Boston and go to the museum and library.

11:30–12:00: Ran into my closest friend Jill. We left the library and sat down on grass in front of one of the dorms. Had a great time talking. Our friends James and Adam joined us after a while. They're very funny.

12:00–1:30 P.M.: Thank goodness the cafeteria opened! Had lunch with everyone. I didn't like the looks of the hamburgers. Too overcooked. Had a big chef salad instead.

1:30–2:20 P.M.: French class. Had a pop quiz. We had to translate a poem we'd never seen before. I did well, but made an appointment with the professor to talk about the last paper. Wasn't happy with my grade. I thought the paper deserved better.

2:20–3:30 P.M.: Ran back to the dorm to change into tennis gear. I'm on the team and need to practice. Had arranged with one of the better players to hit with me for an hour so I didn't want to be late.

3:30–5:45 P.M.: Back to the dorm again. Showered, then sat down in my room with a book on Italian Renaissance and my abnormal-psychology textbook. I think ab psych is my favorite course—it's so interesting! My roommate, Ann, came in, and when I told her I was trying to catch up, she sat down too and started to study. It was kind of nice. Usually one of us wants to study and one of us doesn't, so someone ends up leaving the room.

6:00–6:30 P.M.: Walked with Ann to dinner. She went and sat with her friends and I joined mine. Ate quickly. Had to go down to the gym where the college musical club is rehearsing *A Funny Thing Happened on the Way to the Forum*. Am one of the rehearsal pianists. They really need me. It feels great.

6:45–9:30 P.M.: At rehearsal. Tons of fun. Have a real crush on one of the actors. I think I caught him staring at me last rehearsal. The director (he's a senior) got annoyed at everyone, cast and crew, and said we weren't taking the show seriously enough. Don't think that's true. It's just been a long day.

9:30 P.M.: One of the guys in the cast walked me back to the dorm. (Not all that safe to be out alone at night.) We talked about a girl who just broke up with him. He was very depressed, and I tried to cheer him up. Don't think I helped much.

10:00 P.M.: Ann not back. Turned on some music and started flipping through the latest issue of *People* magazine. Fifteen minutes later climbed into bed and fell asleep. Didn't hear her come in.

College is a place where you will make a lot of decisions on your own. But you are not alone. And that's the key. No matter what the issue or problem, first you have yourself to find a solution. But if that doesn't work, there are plenty of other people to help and guide you. You may be living outside the family you grew up with, but you are living with a new one made up of everyone in the college community. And you are at least as important to this new family as they are to you.

HOMESICKNESS

Most college students experience homesickness on and off during the four years. Freshmen can feel particularly lonesome at first. Everything is so new. On one hand it's terribly exciting, and on the other it's terribly overwhelming. A longing for familiar surroundings, smells, and voices is quite common.

> I remember the second night of school I wandered into the bathroom feeling very blue, and from behind the four stalls I could hear at least two people sniffling away. About two weeks later I couldn't even hear myself think because everyone was chattering so loudly!

There is a period of adjustment for almost everyone. College after all is not like home. Those deep, personal attachments are missed. But as soon as you begin to make friends with other students, the painful feelings will disappear. Then all you will be left with are brief moments when you yearn to hear your mother's voice, or a best friend's jokes, or the smell of your favorite dish cooking on the stove. These feelings will probably come and go throughout your college years. Warm and loving experiences tend to do that. In a way they make us sad, and in another way they can make us feel comforted and protected like a cozy soft blanket wrapped around our shoulders.

Most of what you get from the college experience is up to you. It may seem like a very big responsibility, and it is. But more than that, it's a huge opportunity. Going off on your own will give you perhaps your first sense that you can manage your own life . . . that you can make the rules . . . and that you have the strength to make lots of tough decisions all on your own.

College is a time to find your own special niche. *Photo courtesy of The College of William & Mary, Williamsburg, Virginia*

CONCLUSION

You now have the full picture of what college is like. When people start talking about SATs and financial aid and majors and grade-point averages, you will understand what they mean.

But does that mean you should decide now which, if any, college will be in your future? *Absolutely not!* The most important thing to do now is concentrate on your life. Pursue the things that interest you, take your academic responsibilities seriously, and have a good time.

You're growing and changing a lot now. But you will do that in college too, so why not consider these years good practice? As you have seen, life gets a lot more complicated once you become a college student. If you start taking charge of yourself now, you will be well prepared for the challenge!

Just try and be the best you can be. No one—not you, your friends, your parents, or college—can ask for anything more.

BIBLIOGRAPHY

Activities Booklet. Published by Columbia College, School of Engineering & Applied Science, August 1986, New York.

Admissions Bulletin of Wake Forest University. Published by Wake Forest University, Volume 81, No. 4, August 1986, Winston-Salem, North Carolina.

Antioch University Catalog, 1986–87, Yellow Springs, Ohio.

Berger, Joseph. "Success Strategies for Minorities." *The New York Times.* Section 4A, August 7, 1988.

Bronx Community College Catalog, 1986–88, Editor: Sharlene Hoberman, Bronx, New York.

Bulletin of the University of Wisconsin—Madison. University Publications, Volume 1986, No. 3, March 1986.

Bulletin of Tufts University. Published by Tufts University, Volume 10, No. 2, May 15, 1986, Medford, Massachusetts.

Columbia College Today. Columbia College, Office of Alumni Affairs and Development, Volume 13, No. 3, Fall 1986, New York.

Greene, Howard, and Minton, Robert. *Scaling the Ivy Wall—12 Winning Steps to College Admission.* Little, Brown & Co., Boston, 1987.

Kenyon College Prospectus, Gambier, Ohio.

Rensselaer Undergraduate Catalog. Published by Rensselaer Polytechnic Institute, Volumber 10, 1986, Troy, New York.

Rhode Island School of Design. Office of Publications R.I.S.D., Volume 72, No. 5, August 1986, Providence.

Santa Cruz, an Ideal Becoming Real. Published by the University of Southern California.

Sarah Lawrence Catalog, Bronxville, New York.

The Insider's Guide to the College, 1987–1988. Compiled and edited by Staff of *The Yale Daily News,* St. Martin's Press, New York, 1986.

The University of Michigan Bulletin. Published by the University of Michigan, Volume 16, No. 11, December 3, 1986, Ann Arbor.

INDEX

About the Author

Meg F. Schneider grew up in New York City and now lives in Westchester County. She attended three undergraduate colleges herself until she found one that was just right, but she believes she got something valuable from each experience.

Ms. Schneider has a master's degree in counseling from Columbia University and has written a number of self-help books for young people.